MARTIN SHERMAN

A MADHOUSE
IN GOA

All rights whatsoever in this play are strictly reserved and application for performance, etc. must be made before rehearsals begin to:

Margaret Ramsay Ltd
14a Goodwin's Court
St. Martins Lane
London WC2N 4LL

No performance may be given unless a licence has been obtained.

First published in 1989 by
Amber Lane Press Ltd
Cheorl House
Church Street
Charlbury, Oxon OX7 3PR
Telephone: 0608 810024

Typeset in Baskerville by
Oxonian Rewley Press Ltd., Oxford

Printed in Great Britain by
Bocardo Press Ltd., Didcot, Oxfordshire

Copyright © Martin Sherman, 1989

ISBN 0 906399 96 3

CHARACTERS

PART ONE: *A Table for a King*

DAVID:	early 20's, American
MRS. HONEY:	early 60's, American
COSTOS:	eighteen, Greek
NIKOS:	30's, Greek

PART TWO: *Keeps Rainin' all the Time*

DANIEL HOSANI:	late 40's, American
OLIVER:	late 40's, British
HEATHER:	late 40's, American
DYLAN:	Heather's son, 19, American
ALIKI:	mid-20's
BARNABY GRACE:	late 20's, American

A Madhouse in Goa was first presented at the Lyric Theatre, Hammersmith on 28th April 1989. It was directed by Robert Allan Ackerman with the following cast:

PART ONE: *A Table for a King*

DAVID:	Rupert Graves
MRS. HONEY:	Vanessa Redgrave
COSTOS:	Ian Sears
NIKOS:	Larry Lamb

PART TWO: *Keeps Rainin' all the Time*

DANIEL HOSANI:	Arthur Dignam
OLIVER:	Larry Lamb
HEATHER:	Vanessa Redgrave
DYLAN:	Ian Sears
ALIKI:	Francesca Folan
BARNABY GRACE:	Rupert Graves

Designed by Ultz
Lighting Design: Gerry Jenkinson
Music (Mabel's Song): Richard Sissons

For
Sue Fleming
and
Philip Magdalany

PART ONE

A Table for a King

Darkness. DAVID*'s voice is heard.*

DAVID: [*voice only*] A star fell on Albania. I saw it. Just a few minutes ago. And across the dark Ionian Sea, riding a cool breeze from the Levant, the heavens dance. The moon, burnt orange, shines like an illuminated teardrop.

[*Pause.*]

Oh shit! What's an illuminated teardrop? What a dreadful sentence. Why do I sit here writing about the Levant? I don't know what the Levant is. Or where. It sounds so romantic, though. If only I wasn't alone. Why do I keep this idiot journal? I have to get out of here. Away from this island. Why did I come to Corfu? Will 1966 go down in history as the summer I chased my melancholy across Europe? Oh! Pretentious! Cross it out! Why can't I write a decent sentence? Do people look at me and laugh? What am I doing here?

The lights rise on the veranda of the Kistos Inn.

A tiny village in Corfu. Summer. 1966.

The inn — small, very white and comfortable, stretches out behind the veranda. The veranda itself is occupied by a number of tables, some of them set for breakfast. A door on one side leads to the kitchen. There are steps on the other side that lead to rocks, which descend, in turn, to the sea that stretches out before the veranda. A group of beach chairs is piled on top of each other near the steps.

It is a blazing hot morning.

MRS. HONEY *sits at the centre table — the largest table and one with a commanding view. She is in her early sixties, American.*

DAVID, *also American, sits at a nearby table. He is in his early twenties. He wears slacks and a long-sleeved shirt, buttoned to the top. His movements are awkward and insecure.*

MRS. HONEY: Waiting! I'm waiting. Hello. I'm waiting!

[COSTOS *walks in from the kitchen, carrying a tray. He is Greek, eighteen, handsome, wearing shorts and a tee-shirt. He is humming 'Yesterday' by The Beatles.*]

Where is Yannis Kistos? Yannis Kistos or his brother Nikos Kistos? The proprietors of the Kistos Inn? I demand to see the Kistos Brothers! Tell them I'm waiting. For my tea.

[COSTOS *puts the contents of his tray — breakfast — on* DAVID's *table. He is still humming.*]

And my toast. For my breakfast.

[COSTOS *walks off with the tray.*]

[*to* DAVID] Glory Hallelujah! I declare . . . this is not a well-run establishment. I'm sure you've noticed. I saw you arrive yesterday morning. Time enough for you to observe how poorly run this establishment is. Sweet Jesus! And yet the Kistos Brothers own a popular inn. Oh yes. Difficult to believe, isn't it? It does supply the most luxurious accommodations on this part of Corfu, but what does this part of Corfu have to offer, I ask you? A few goats, a dirty taverna, a puny village and that dreadful view of the Albanian coast. Have you seen anything *move* on the Albanian coast? I have never even been to Albania. Yes, it is a popular inn, Chez Kistos Frères. Do you know who ate here Friday night? Lawrence Durrell! They wanted me to give up my table for him. This table. Quite the best table. I always insist upon it when I make my reservations. I have been here three times. I suppose it is a very special place, the Casa Kistos, don't you think? Serene. Well — what has he done, I ask you? Lawrence Durrell? Write a quartet. I'm not impressed. You're supposed to compose quartets, I believe, not write them. Have you read it? There's a wonderful hotel in Alexandria and I don't believe he mentions it at all. Of course, by wonderful I mean quite inexpensive but clean. I suppose nobody in his quartet does anything inexpensive. Or clean. Well, well, well, I don't know, I don't know. I did give up my table. Yes, I did. So I do think I deserve breakfast. Lordy — I do.

[*She takes a bell out of her pocket and rings it.*]

Waiting! Call Nikos. Call Yannis. Waiting! I'm waiting! I carry my own bell. It's indispensable. Service is appalling everywhere, don't you think?

[*Pause.*]

We have a great deal in common — you and I — a great deal, well perhaps not a great deal, but one thing. We are both travelling alone. Now I will say this for the Kistos Inn. They have single rooms. Solitary travellers are the most despised race on earth, of course you realize that. It is usually impossible to obtain a single room. I always advised my children to marry at an early age so they would qualify for double rooms. Unfortunately, they listened to me. Unlike this waiter.

[*She rings the bell again.*]

He understands English perfectly. He's just insolent. So — you're a photographer? I saw your camera. It must be very heavy. I suppose that's why you stoop. I noticed your posture at once. What's your name?

[*Pause.*]

DAVID: David.

MRS. HONEY: Now *that* is a fine hotel. The King David. In Jerusalem. Are you Jewish?

DAVID: Yes.

MRS. HONEY: Lordy. An artist *and* a Jew. I do hope you're homosexual
as well, they all three seem to complement each other,
don't they? I, of course, didn't grow up with any Jews,
not in Mississippi. I met them later, a few, on my
travels. Where are those siblings? Nikos? Yannis!
Will you take my photograph? I long to have my
photograph taken. At *my* dinner table. Perhaps
L. Durrell has left his spirit at the table. Perhaps it
will materialize on film. Oh — please — will you?

DAVID: Well . . . I'm not very . . .

MRS. HONEY: It will be an adventure, won't it? I did have my photograph taken in Calcutta once. I had just purchased a
camera. I thought my children should have a record of
my travels. I asked a sweet little beggar to take my
picture. I paid him, of course — he must have been
terribly hungry and he had a stoop, just like yours,
and only two fingers, one on each hand, which made
it difficult to hold the camera, but marvel of marvels,
he focused the thing and clicked it too, and then
smiled the most wonderful smile and ran off with the
camera. I tried chasing him but I think his two fingers
gave him extra speed. It always helps to travel light.
That, of course, was before I realized my children
were not interested in seeing photographs. I wonder if
he still has the camera? I have wondered, in the clear
light of retrospect, you understand, if he was a leper.
I've always had a morbid fear of lepers. Now where
would a leper get a roll of film developed? I won't say
that question has haunted me, but I *have* wondered . . .
I think it's fair to say his stoop was a permanent
stance. So you will — won't you — take my photograph? Please say yes.

DAVID: Well . . . [*smiles*] Yes.

MRS. HONEY: Thank you. Now, if only I can get breakfast. You seem
to have yours.

          [*She rings the bell again.*]

I must confess, the bell is hopeless. Never gets me
anything. Still . . .

          [*She rings it again, vigorously.*]

Waiting! I'm waiting. Sweet Jesus, I'm waiting!

          [*The lights fade.*]

[DAVID*'s voice is heard.*]

DAVID: [*voice only*] I met an amazing woman this morning. On the veranda, waiting for breakfast. Her name is Mrs. Honey and she is from Mississippi and she travels all over the world and she never stops talking and I promised to take her photograph. Now why did I do that? I'm so stupid. I *am* stupid. And lonely. And sad. And confused and ugly and desperate. Why am I here?

[*His voice fades off.*]

The lights rise on the veranda. Afteroon. It is very hot.

DAVID *is fidgeting with his camera. The camera is very old and a classic of its kind, resting on a tripod and using plates to record its images. It has a hood to cover the photographer when he wants to check the light.* DAVID *also has a small portable light-meter in his hand.*

MRS. HONEY *is sitting at her table, wearing a very light cotton dress, her eyes closed, absorbing the sun.*

MRS. HONEY: I feel like I'm under water. Floating. Not real. In a different time.

[*She opens her eyes.*]

That camera — my husband, the dentist, had one just like it. Many years ago. Is it an antique?

DAVID: I don't know. It takes the best . . .

MRS. HONEY: I can't hear you.

[*She closes her eyes again.*]

[COSTOS *enters, carrying a tray. He grins at* DAVID. DAVID, *embarrassed, ducks underneath the hood.* COSTOS *walks through the veranda, humming 'Homeward Bound' by Paul Simon. He walks off.* DAVID *comes out of the hood.*]

DAVID: It takes the best . . .

[NIKOS *enters. He is Greek, in his thirties, and wears shorts and a tee-shirt. His English is only lightly accented. He carries a deck of cards. He sits at a table near* MRS. HONEY *and starts to play solitaire.*]

NIKOS: A photographic session?

[MRS. HONEY *opens her eyes.*]

Nikos! Yes — indeed. You have a distinguished guest.
A famous photographer.

DAVID: [*embarrassed*] No, I'm just . . .

NIKOS: We have many distinguished guests here. This *is* the
finest inn on this part of the island. It was very kind of
you to give up your table for Mr. Durrell.

MRS. HONEY: Well — he is an artist. Artists make things grow.

NIKOS: [*losing at solitaire*] Son-of-a-bitch!
[DAVID *is circling them with the light-meter.*]

MRS. HONEY: Nikos, you're in the light. Surely he's in the light.

DAVID: No. It's fine.

NIKOS: I am in the way?

DAVID: No.

MRS. HONEY: Of course you're in the way. Nikos went to Oxford.

DAVID: Really?

MRS. HONEY: I find, in general, that if you've been to Oxford, you're
in the way. Of course, I can't imagine why he and his
invisible brother run a hotel in such an insignificant
village. Can you? Speak up, child.

DAVID: Well, I don't . . .

NIKOS: Now, my dear Mrs. Honey — I must ask you for
another favour.
[*He hits his cards.*]
Bloody hell.

MRS. HONEY: You play solitaire with such passion.

NIKOS: It is not a sad game, not a lonely game, Mrs. Honey.
Not for a Greek.
[DAVID *stands next to the camera, holding a small switch
connected by wire to the camera.*]

DAVID: Now!

MRS. HONEY: What?
[DAVID *presses the button.*]

DAVID: There.

MRS. HONEY: Oh. I had my picture took.

DAVID: [*removing the frame*] I liked the look on your . . .

MRS. HONEY: Imperious?

DAVID: Yes.

NIKOS: Another favour. [*to his cards*] There. That's better.

MRS. HONEY: What did you study at Oxford?

NIKOS: Political science.

MRS. HONEY: But that's meaningless. Especially in Greece.

NIKOS: That's why I run a hotel. [*to his cards*] Beautiful.

MRS. HONEY:	[*to* DAVID] Take another photograph. With Nikos.
DAVID:	Yes?
MRS. HONEY:	The two of us.
NIKOS:	No.
MRS. HONEY:	Yes. Please. You would like that?
DAVID:	I would.
MRS. HONEY:	Speak up, child.
DAVID:	I mumble. I'm sorry.
MRS. HONEY:	You what?
DAVID:	Mumble.

[*He circles them again with his light-meter.*]

MRS. HONEY:	Well, yes, you swallow your words. So did the dentist. Too much saliva, he said. I'd say a miserable childhood. Which would explain your clothing. You're so overdressed. It's blazing hot, isn't it? My, my, you're buttoned. What is the temperature, Nikos?
NIKOS:	I must ask you . . .
MRS. HONEY:	Oh, Nikos, ask not, ask not. Come — have your picture took too. Leave those silly cards. It is a lonely game, no matter what you say. I used to play it endlessly. While the dentist was dying. It's a game for *that*. Stand here. Put your arm around me. Host and guest. Milk and Honey.
NIKOS:	If it pleases you. [*rises*] Where?
MRS. HONEY:	Right here. [*motions by her side*] Do you like this, dear?
DAVID:	Closer.
MRS. HONEY:	Pardon?
DAVID:	*Closer.*
MRS. HONEY:	Swallow all the saliva and then speak. Closer, Nikos. Just stand still. He has to run around with that silly little thing and focus. You're a handsome man, Nikos. Nice legs. The dentist's legs were appalling.
NIKOS:	Tomorrow evening, my dear Mrs. Honey . . .
MRS. HONEY:	Oh Nikos, you're so single-minded. Don't you ever ramble?
NIKOS:	There is a special guest coming for dinner.
MRS. HONEY:	When?
NIKOS:	Tomorrow evening.
MRS. HONEY:	Oh. You said that.
NIKOS:	Yes.
MRS. HONEY:	Well, that's nice. I hope he enjoys it. Will you be serving something with lamb?

NIKOS: I must ask you . . .

MRS. HONEY: You mustn't, you mustn't. Don't talk. He doesn't want your mouth to move.

DAVID: It's alright. I'm not ready.
[*He ducks under the hood.*]

MRS. HONEY: I think he said he's not ready. The child mumbles. He's also very slow. But I'm sure he wants to get your legs into the shot. Actually — in truth — I rarely saw the dentist's legs.

NIKOS: I must ask you to give up your table once again.

MRS. HONEY: I always had excellent diction. Never mumbled. You ask too much.

NIKOS: For one evening only.

MRS. HONEY: One evening too many.

NIKOS: It is a special favour.

MRS. HONEY: It is *my* table. Mine. It has the best view. Of the olive trees. Of the beach. Of the sea. Of that empty little rowboat in the water. Of Albania. I come to this hotel because of the view of Albania.

NIKOS: I am serious.

MRS. HONEY: I am too. About the table. I do reserve this table, as well as my room, four months in advance. Do any of your other clients do that? I seriously doubt it.

NIKOS: This guest is very special.
[DAVID *comes out from under the hood.*]

MRS. HONEY: [*to* DAVID] Aren't you ready yet?

DAVID: Almost.

MRS. HONEY: I'm sorry.

DAVID: *Almost.*

MRS. HONEY: Almost. More special than Mr. Durrell?

NIKOS: Yes.

MRS. HONEY: Has he written a quintet, then? Lordy, this insignificant village is crawling with great artists.

DAVID: *Almost ready.*

MRS. HONEY: You needn't shout. The dentist was the same way, if he wasn't mumbling, he was shouting. Smile, Nikos. Tell me, who is this very special guest? Is it Mr. Auden or Mr. Stravinsky or, gracious me, Mr. Picasso? Are they all rushing to Corfu? Do they think the view of Albania might inspire them?

NIKOS: I could choke you, Mrs. Honey.

[MRS. HONEY *laughs.* DAVID *stands next to the camera, holding the switch.*]

DAVID: Now.

MRS. HONEY: What?

DAVID: I said now.

MRS. HONEY: Oh. Now. Now, Nikos. Smile. Just imagine your hands around my neck, and smile.

[NIKOS *breaks into a broad smile.*]

NIKOS: He is not an artist.

MRS. HONEY: Then he doesn't deserve a table.

NIKOS: He is a king.

DAVID: [*presses the switch*] Got it.

MRS. HONEY: A king!

[DAVID *quickly turns the plate over and replaces it in the camera.*]

DAVID: One more.

MRS. HONEY: Goodness — dime a dozen.

DAVID: This one will be faster.

MRS. HONEY: You meet kings and princes and dukes everywhere these days. Running around without their countries, looking for a free meal. Where is this one from?

DAVID: Can you smile again?

NIKOS: From here.

MRS. HONEY: Here?

DAVID: Please?

NIKOS: Yes. Here.

MRS. HONEY: Greece?

NIKOS: Greece.

DAVID: Please!

MRS. HONEY: Sorry?

DAVID: Say cheese.

MRS. HONEY: Why?

DAVID: [*presses the switch*] Thank you.

MRS. HONEY: Oh, Nikos. Well, well, well. So it's that King. Your King. This King. *The* King. Dining at the Kistos Inn?

NIKOS: He has a home nearby.

MRS. HONEY: With Mr. Durrell? Are they lovers? Oh, you Greeks are so sly. Does the King come here for your legs?

NIKOS: Choke.

MRS. HONEY: [*to* DAVID] Take one of Nikos — by himself.

NIKOS: No — no — no.

[*He moves away and sits at his table again and resumes his game of solitaire.*]

MRS. HONEY: Nikos is obviously more important than he seems. Oh, Nikos, Nikos.

[*Pause.*]

No. I won't give up the table.

NIKOS: You can sit at my table.

MRS. HONEY: It's too far away. It's near the kitchen. It attracts Greek mosquitoes.

NIKOS: You can sit with the honeymoon couple.

MRS. HONEY: *With* them?

NIKOS: I'll put them with the Germans.

MRS. HONEY: That would destroy their marriage. So would I. I have a wicked tongue. No, no.

NIKOS: You can sit with the French scientist.

MRS. HONEY: He'll talk to me. In *French*. No, no.

NIKOS: You can sit with your friend here.

[*He points to* DAVID, *who is dismantling the camera.*]

MRS. HONEY: The child likes his solitude.

DAVID: I don't really mind . . .

MRS. HONEY: He wants to be alone with his thoughts. He's happy that way. Alone. No, no, no. The King will have to sit with the Germans or the French scientist or even with you, although, if you did study political science, I don't think you would have anything to say to him. No, Nikos, I won't give up my table. If he were an artist, like Mr. Durrell . . . then I'd grumble and I'd protest, but in the end, I'd graciously give in. But a King! A politician! He has blood on his hands, Nikos. Quite simply that. On some level — even if he's a nice young chap — he's a killer. You must know that. You studied that. A murderer. Oh, let him go to the local taverna. Let him dine with his deeply distressed subjects. But this table — is mine.

[*Pause.*]

NIKOS: I must have it.

MRS. HONEY: Mine.

NIKOS: I *will* have it.

[*He throws the cards off the table and stands up.*]

MRS. HONEY: I've paid for it.

NIKOS: [*smiles*] We've just killed each other not too long ago,

Mrs. Honey. My people. Brother against brother. As they say. We watched each other die.

[*Pause.*]

A Greek isn't a Greek if he tells the truth. Pardon my lapse. For this is the truth. I will have the table.

[*He kisses* MRS. HONEY *on her forehead.*]

Dear lady. I always enjoy your visits here.

[NIKOS *leaves.*]

[*Silence.*]

MRS. HONEY: Smooth. Don't you think?

DAVID: I don't know.

MRS. HONEY: Too smooth. There's a story there. How does a Greek boy from Corfu get to Oxford? Where did he learn perfect English? Why does he run a hotel? And where on earth is the other one, his brother? Oh, there is a story there. And we will never know it, you and I, we will never know it. When we travel, we pick up impressions, that's all. Never the truth. We're never invited inside.

[*Pause.*]

You and I.

[*Pause.*]

Will they be pretty photographs?

DAVID: I hope.

MRS. HONEY: Are you pleased?

DAVID: I think so.

MRS. HONEY: Aren't you hot? All those buttons.

DAVID: No.

MRS. HONEY: I have very little in life, you see. The dentist is dead. The children don't need or want me. I see deceit everywhere. I have very little. Occasionally, in some insignificant village, in some country I barely know, I have a table. Do you understand? Why are you so quiet? Look at your hair. It just sits there. You must give it some *style*.

[*She runs her finger through his hair, messing it up, trying to give it some body.*]

Someday, you will understand.

[*The lights fade.*]

[DAVID's *voice is heard.*]

DAVID: [*voice only*] Why did I bring this awful camera? No one travels with a camera like this. It's so heavy. The plates weigh a ton. Why do I think I can take photographs? When I try to carry the camera *and* the suitcase together, it's a living hell. I keep throwing clothing away, to make the suitcase lighter. It never gets lighter. It's a nightmare. The suitcase keeps brushing against my leg. And now the skin is falling off my leg. I have a rash on my arm as well. And my stomach hurts all the time. Maybe I'm dying. I think that I'm dying. What am I doing here?

[*His voice trails away.*]

The lights rise.

The veranda. Evening.

DAVID *is sitting at the table, writing in his journal.* MRS. HONEY *enters, wearing a nightgown. She is carrying a bottle of wine and two small glasses.*

MRS. HONEY: Sweet Jesus! What an evening. Do you hear a cow out there? I have some wine. And glasses. I couldn't sleep. I saw you on the veranda. I had waking dreams, do you know them? Amazing landscapes, but one eye is open. Cows are much too noisy. Nikos Kistos has invaded my dreams. Manically chopping my table up with an axe. Here.

[*She sits at her table.*]

Move over here, to the table in question.

[DAVID *joins her at her table.*]

They've waxed it. See? Have some retsina. It tastes like nail polish. I don't drink too often. But this evening . . . well . . . it just isn't right, some evenings aren't, out there — in the world — not right . . .

[*She pours him a glass of wine.*]

DAVID: [*takes the glass*] Thank you.

MRS. HONEY: Drink it down very fast. Nikos Kistos is an evil man, mind my words, he's planning something. I smell enemies. I do, I do. Mind my words.

DAVID: [*drinks his wine*] Oh, my God.

MRS. HONEY: A bit like lava, isn't it? Have another.

[*She pours him another glass.*]

Glory be, child, don't you want to unbutton something?

DAVID: [*drinks the wine*] Ohh!

MRS. HONEY: [*drinks her wine*] It's good for you. Go on. Another.

DAVID: I can't.

MRS. HONEY: I insist.

DAVID: Well . . .

> [*She pours him another glass.*]

O.K. [*giggles*] It tastes awful. [*drinks the wine*] Do you, do you, do you . . . ?

MRS. HONEY: What?

DAVID: Do you . . . ?

> [*He pauses for breath.*]

MRS. HONEY: Speak up, child.

DAVID: Do you know where the Levant is?

MRS. HONEY: Oh. Somewhere, dear. Definitely somewhere. Somewhere out there. [*drinks her wine*] We're not savouring this, are we?

> [*She pours DAVID another glass.*]

Something to do with the Mediterranean. Places like Cyprus . . . Syria . . . Lebanon . . .

DAVID: [*drinks his wine*] Jesus!

MRS. HONEY: Do you know Beirut? That's probably part of the Levant. You must go there someday. It's an absolute jewel. I travel, you know — place to place to place . . .

> [*She pours herself another glass.*]

My, this stuff grows on you. I'm never anywhere for too long. They know my name at every American Express office in Europe and Asia. Not Australia. Doesn't interest me. I have this table reserved for another ten days. Damn Nikos Kistos! I don't want to move. [*drinks the wine*] A tiny bit more?

> [*She pours another glass.*]

Well. Beirut. Now, I'm not partial to nightclubs but in Beirut nightclubs are as natural as the sea. There's one that is, in fact, by the sea; it has a spectacular if rather grotesque stage show and, for a finale, a long, giant, life-size train winds its way across the nightclub floor, weaving around the tables, with chorus girls standing on top of the railway cars, and cages coming down from the ceiling, those too with chorus girls, and flowers raining down on the tables, and gold coins as well, falling past the chorus girls in the cages onto the chorus girls on the train.

                [DAVID *looks at her, dumbfounded.*]
Lordy! What a silly thing to remember. Well. Beirut.
                [*She holds her glass up in a toast.*]

DAVID: [*holds his glass up*] Beirut.

MRS. HONEY: The glass is empty. I do get fond of certain places. Usually much later. After I've left. I'll give you the address of a lovely hotel there. And that nightclub. You will go there some day. On your travels. Nikos Kistos worries me, boy.

DAVID: I'm sick of my travels.

MRS. HONEY: He wants this table, he does. It's only a piece of wood. Such a fuss.

DAVID: I'm sick of my travels.

MRS. HONEY: And he's devious. And it's a King. Spells trouble.

DAVID: I'm sick of my travels.

MRS. HONEY: What? Oh. Which travels?

DAVID: These. Here. There. This summer. My summer in Europe.
                [*Pause.*]

MRS. HONEY: Where have you been?

DAVID: Everywhere.

MRS. HONEY: For instance?

DAVID: Paris.

MRS. HONEY: [*smiles*] Ah!

DAVID: It was horrible.

MRS. HONEY: Oh.

DAVID: London.

MRS. HONEY: Ummm.

DAVID: A nightmare.

MRS. HONEY: I see.

DAVID: Rome.

MRS. HONEY: Roma!

DAVID: I hated it.

MRS. HONEY: Hated it?

DAVID: Venice.

MRS. HONEY: Miserable?

DAVID: Miserable.

MRS. HONEY: [*laughs*] I think you need these last few drops . . .
                [*She empties the dregs of the wine bottle into his glass.*]

DAVID: Why is it so funny?

MRS. HONEY: Did you not find Venice a little, a bit, a tiny bit — itsy-bitsy bit — beautiful?

[*She laughs again.*]

DAVID: Yes.

MRS. HONEY: Then why was it miserable?

DAVID: I don't know. Yes, I do. You see, it was me. I was . . .

MRS. HONEY: What?

DAVID: Nothing.

MRS. HONEY: Go on.

DAVID: No.

MRS. HONEY: Spit it out. [*laughs*] I used to say that to the dentist, spit it out. Of course, he said the same thing to his patients. I wonder who picked it up from whom.
[*Pause.*]

DAVID: I was lonely.

MRS. HONEY: [*laughs*] Oh. I'm sorry. I have a laughing fit. I don't mean it. Glory be! Lonely? Dear, dear.

DAVID: No one has talked to me. You're the first person on this entire trip who has talked to me.

MRS. HONEY: It's all those buttons. You're so covered up. You do not invite conversation. I'm amazed you're not wearing a necktie. Are your parents the very religious type? Do they abhor the human body? I have heard that Orthodox Jews make love through a hole in the sheet — is that true of your parents? — and if so, do they tear a hole or is it meticulously cut? Well, well, well — you are not a happy specimen, are you? Still in school?

DAVID: Just out. Out. Into the darkness . . .
[*He stands up — can't handle it — sits down again.*]

MRS. HONEY: And child, your hair. It's so homeless. Did you notice, in London, during your nightmare stay there, that some of the young men are now wearing their hair long and wild and quite beautiful? Let your hair grow, boy. And muss it a bit. And treat yourself to sideburns. And slash away your trousers. Yes — show us your legs. Do you have a shape to you? Let's see it, child.

DAVID: I'm drowning.

MRS. HONEY: Oh dear.

DAVID: I'm tottering . . .

MRS. HONEY: You're drunk.

DAVID: On the edge . . .

MRS. HONEY: Very drunk.

DAVID: Of an abyss!
             [MRS. HONEY *stares at him and starts to laugh again.*]
MRS. HONEY: I'm sorry.
DAVID: I don't have nice legs.
             [*He starts to cry.*]
             I'm drunk. Michael! Do you have more wine? My legs
             are scrawny. My kneecaps stick out. He doesn't love
             me at all. He lied to me.
MRS. HONEY: Shh! You will wake the hotel up. Nikos Kistos will
             have us arrested for drinking. He's planning some-
             thing, Nikos Kistos. The King could order a firing
             squad.
DAVID: I'm burning!
MRS. HONEY: It's the sun. It was extremely strong this afternoon.
DAVID: I'm on fire.
MRS. HONEY: Or then again, he could try to poison me.
DAVID: I'm lost in an inferno!
             [MRS. HONEY *looks up.*]
MRS. HONEY: [*sharply*] Inferno? Dear, dear. Retsina, you old dog.
             Now, let's pull ourselves together.
DAVID: I'm so unhappy. I want to die! I want to join a kibbutz!
MRS. HONEY: Well, at least you have a sense of priority.
DAVID: I'm twenty-three . . .
MRS. HONEY: *That* old!
DAVID: So much of me has been washed away . . .
MRS. HONEY: You tend to over-dramatize, did you know that? Is
             that why you take photographs? Are you attracted to
             the theatre? Do you have any friends?
DAVID: I'm falling . . . falling . . .
MRS. HONEY: Oh, I'm no good at this. Mothering.
DAVID: Into the abyss . . .
MRS. HONEY: Never suited me. Ask my children. They loathe me for
             good reason.
DAVID: The abyss . . .
MRS. HONEY: No, child. It's not an inferno. It's not even a brushfire.
             It's not an abyss. Do you know what an abyss is?
DAVID: What?
MRS. HONEY: Watching the dentist disappear before your eyes.
             Cancer. That's an abyss. Watching his flesh melt
             away from his face. Watching a truck drive through
             his body every night. That's an abyss. Now dry your

eyes and go to bed. We mustn't wake the evil Kistos up. The Kisti. Where is his brother?

[*She stands up and looks at the sea.*]

Not being loved is nothing. Easy. Fact of life. The dentist didn't love me, certainly not after the first year, but then, I never stopped jabbering, so who can blame him? And I didn't love the dentist, he was a fairly tedious man, although that is no reason to die such a cruel death. No, I married him to get away from my parents' home, and I did, God knows, I did. He took me to Utah, to the desert, the clean, quiet empty desert, which, believe it or not, I much preferred to Mississippi. And I liked his last name. To be called Honey in perpetuity. Who could resist? And when he finally met his humourless maker I found I had nothing to do. But stare at the desert. The dentist was a companion, you see. He rarely spoke, and when he did it was usually about bleeding gums, but still, he was there, sitting next to me, boring me, but not with malice, and we took comfort in being bored together. But left alone, I was useless. All I was trained to do in Mississippi was to read magazines and chatter. My children fled from my endless chatter. My daughter married a man every bit as dull as the dentist, isn't that always the way? And my son, who has some spunk and brains, moved as far away as he could. They were both petrified I'd visit them, so they suggested I take a trip. I packed a suitcase. It's been four years and I'll never return. They send me money every few months. To American Express. And now I chatter in different locations for a few weeks at a time. And move on. And that, too, is an abyss.

DAVID: I'm embarrassed, I didn't mean to . . .

MRS. HONEY: My son sent a letter with his last cheque. He's left his job. He's heading for San Francisco with his wife. He says the world is changing. There's a new kind of life. He says. He has *hope*. Well. Glory Hallelujah, bless his soul. *And* — his hair is very long. He sent a photograph. I think he looks quite stunning. He's not much older than you.

[*She brushes* DAVID's *hair.*]

Please. Let it grow.
[*Pause.*]
Well, well, well. Time to return Nikos Kistos to my dreams. Time to close my eyes and see him pulling at my table, like a demented puppy. Down, Nikos, down!
[*She brushes her hand across his face.*]
Breathe a little. Let some fresh air in. Throw away your camera. Forget your hurt. Forget your family. Buy some shorts. Have adventures. But first — go to sleep. Sleep is good for growing hair.
[*She kisses him. He stares at her.*]

DAVID: Mrs. Honey?

MRS. HONEY: What?

DAVID: Your nightgown — is on upside down.

MRS. HONEY: Well, so it is. Fancy that.
[*She leaves.*]

[DAVID *sits alone at the table. He runs his hand through his hair and starts to pull on it, as if to make it grow.*]

[*Silence.*]

[COSTOS *enters, from the beach. He is wearing a bathing suit. A beach-blanket hangs over his shoulder. He sees* DAVID. *He smiles. He starts to hum 'Strangers in the Night'.* DAVID *looks up at* COSTOS, *startled. He sees* COSTOS *smile and smiles back tentatively, then turns away.* COSTOS *walks into the kitchen.*]

[DAVID *gathers his notebook, the two glasses and the empty wine bottle and starts to leave. He is a bit unsteady on his feet. He looks for some place to throw the bottle.*]

[COSTOS *re-enters, carrying a large glass of water.* DAVID *stops, transfixed by* COSTOS' *body.*]

COSTOS: Water.

DAVID: What?

COSTOS: You wanted water?

DAVID: No.

COSTOS: Glass of water.

DAVID: No.

COSTOS: I make mistake?

DAVID: Yes.

COSTOS: Think you want water.

DAVID: No.

[*Pause.* DAVID *starts to leave again.*]

COSTOS: I bring it to your room.

DAVID: Bring what?

COSTOS: Water.

DAVID: No.

COSTOS: Room number six?

DAVID: Yes.

COSTOS: I bring it.

DAVID: I don't want water.

COSTOS: I was going to bring at any rate.

DAVID: You were?

COSTOS: After I swim. Tonight. To room six. To you.

DAVID: You were?

COSTOS: Yes.

DAVID: Why?

COSTOS: But now you here. Better. So drink it here.

    [*He holds out the glass.*]

DAVID: But I don't want . . .

    [COSTOS *stares at him.*]

    Well . . . I suppose . . .

    [*He takes the glass.*]

    Thank you.

COSTOS: You see. I know what you want.

DAVID: It's only water.

COSTOS: Drink it.

    [*Pause.*]

DAVID: Alright.

    [*He drinks the water.*]

COSTOS: Is good?

DAVID: Yes.

COSTOS: Greek water is good?

DAVID: Excellent.

COSTOS: You know Barbara Ann?

DAVID: Who?

COSTOS: Barbara Ann.

DAVID: No.

COSTOS: Song. By Beach Boys.

DAVID: Oh. Oh! I see. Beach Boys. No. I don't listen to . . .

COSTOS: I'm still wet. From sea. Dry under stars. Here. Take chairs.

    [*He goes to the side of the veranda where the beach chairs are piled up and drags two to the centre of the veranda.*]

You help me.

> [DAVID *helps him with the chairs.*]

Good. We lie down.

> [COSTOS *throws his blanket on one of the chairs and lies on it, stretching out, provocatively.* DAVID *stares at him.*]

Go on. You too.

> [DAVID *doesn't move.* COSTOS — *impatient* — *taps the chair next to him.*]

Here. Here. Under stars.

> [*Pause.*]

DAVID: Why not?

> [*He lies down on the other chair.*]

My God! [*staring at the sky*] Look at them.

COSTOS: Tomorrow big day.

DAVID: Is it?

COSTOS: King is here.

DAVID: I know.

COSTOS: We have good King.

DAVID: Yes.

COSTOS: No King in America.

DAVID: No. So many stars. I feel almost . . .

COSTOS: Greece happy with King . . .

DAVID: Almost . . .

COSTOS: King is like father.

DAVID: Almost someplace else.

COSTOS: You know Sergeant Barry Sadler?

DAVID: Who?

COSTOS: 'Ballad of Green Berets'. War song. Big hit. Vietnam. You like it?

DAVID: I don't know it.

COSTOS: No wars in Greece any more. You know this —? [*sings*] 'Under the boardwalk, we'll be fallin' in love. Under the boardwalk, boardwalk.'

DAVID: No.

COSTOS: Drifters.

DAVID: Oh. I see.

COSTOS: Move chairs closer.

> [*He reaches out and pulls* DAVID'S *chair directly next to his, then puts his arm on* DAVID'S *shoulder.*]

I know what you want. I have many brains. I go to university next year. You go to university?

DAVID: I did.

COSTOS: You leave.

DAVID: Graduate.

COSTOS: You smart person too. You study with the camera?

DAVID: A little. Yes.

COSTOS: I can tell. Smart person. Take pictures for money?

DAVID: Not yet. Someday.

COSTOS: [*sings*] 'Cool cat, lookin' for a kitty. Gonna look in every corner of the city.' Know that?

DAVID: No.

COSTOS: Lovin' Spoonful.

DAVID: I never listen to contemporary . . .

COSTOS: [*sings*] 'And baby, if the music is right, I'll meet you tomorrow, sort of late at night.'
[*Pause.*]
How I learn my English, Sonny. Cher. Mamas. Papas. Simon. Garfunkel. Good teachers. My English good?

DAVID: Very.
[COSTOS *moves his arm past* DAVID*'s shoulder and lays it on* DAVID*'s chest.*]

COSTOS: You have girlfriend?

DAVID: No.

COSTOS: I have many.

DAVID: Oh.

COSTOS: Boyfriends too.
[*Pause.*]

DAVID: Oh.
[COSTOS *starts to caress* DAVID*'s chest.*]

COSTOS: You have boyfriends?

DAVID: No.

COSTOS: Not even one?
[*Pause.*]

DAVID: No.

COSTOS: You not serious.

DAVID: I am. Serious. No. [*sits up*] I think I am going to sleep now. [*rises*] I'm just a little drunk.
[COSTOS *grabs* DAVID*'s legs.*]

COSTOS: You stay.

DAVID: I can't.

COSTOS: What make you drunk?

DAVID: Retsina.

COSTOS: It is good, retsina?

DAVID: Yes. But bitter.

COSTOS: Bitter — good?

DAVID: Yes. Bitter very good. But too much. I feel strange.

COSTOS: You feel happy?

DAVID: Happy? No! No happy.
[*Pause.*]
Strange.

COSTOS: Strange — good?

DAVID: I don't know. I can't answer.
[COSTOS *pulls* DAVID *down to his chair.*]
What are you doing?

COSTOS: Look at stars. Beautiful. Greek night. Sound of waves. Magic. I know what you want. I have many brains. I will go to university. I'll be smart person too. [*sings*] 'We'll sing in the sunshine. We'll laugh everyday.' Know that?

DAVID: No.

COSTOS: Gale Garnett. Big hit. No sunshine now. Stars.
[*He brushes his hand across* DAVID's *mouth.*]

DAVID: Stars.

COSTOS: It is very hot, no?

DAVID: Yes.
[COSTOS *takes* DAVID's *hand and places it on his chest, then sings.*]

COSTOS: 'Then I'll be on my way.'
[*Pause.*]
I am very hot. You also?

DAVID: Yes.

COSTOS: Why you never unbutton?
[*He moves* DAVID's *hand across his chest.*]
Greece very hot. You like Greece?
[*He puts* DAVID's *hand on his nipple.*]

DAVID: Very much.

COSTOS: You think Greece beautiful?

DAVID: Very.

COSTOS: Unbutton.
[*He starts to unbutton* DAVID's *shirt.*]

DAVID: No.
[*He sits up.*]

COSTOS: What is wrong?

DAVID: Nothing.

COSTOS: I want to look at you.

DAVID: You do? Really?

COSTOS: Yes. Sure. [*sings*] 'And it's magic, if the music is groovy.'

DAVID: Everybody wants me to unbutton. But I don't . . . Oh. What the hell.

[*He pulls his shirt open.*]

Unbuttoned! Oh God, I think I tore it. I tore my shirt. This is a catastrophe.

COSTOS: Leave open.

DAVID: I only have a few shirts with me. And this one drip-dries and . . .

COSTOS: Like shirt torn. Sexy.

DAVID: Sexy?

COSTOS: Yes.

DAVID: Really?

COSTOS: Really.

DAVID: Me? No . . .

COSTOS: Your skin so white. No beach?

DAVID: No beach, no. Can't swim. I visit ruins. No beach. My family . . . they think modern bathing suits are . . . Oh, that's silly . . . I don't listen to them anyway . . . I . . . can't swim though . . .

COSTOS: [*sings*] 'Hey Mr. Tambourine Man, Sing a song for me.' I know what you want. I have many brains.

[*He pulls DAVID's shirt completely open.*]

DAVID: It's cold. There's a draught.

COSTOS: It's hot. [*sings*] 'Hot-town, summer in the city.'

[*Pause.*]

Put hand here . . .

[*He places DAVID's hand on his crotch.*]

[*sings*] 'I'm not sleepy and there's no place I'm going to.'

[*He pulls DAVID down.*]

Lips here.

[*He kisses DAVID.*]

[*DAVID pulls himself up. COSTOS pulls him down again, and as he does so takes the beach blanket out from under his body and drapes it over them, covering both of their bodies.*]

Here. I make you relax. You like blanket? Pretty Greek blanket. There. Now you do not have to look. Just feel. Better. I have many brains. I know what you want.

[*There is now much mutual activity underneath the blanket.*]

	You like?
DAVID:	Yes. I like.
COSTOS:	Very much?
DAVID:	Very much.
COSTOS:	[*sings*] 'In the jingle-jangle morning, I'll come following you.'

[*He speaks in a murmur as he explores* DAVID'*s body.*]

COSTOS: Do you feel the jingle-jangle? You come following through under the boardwalks? What a day for a day-dream. All my thoughts are far away. Do you believe in magic? Homeward bound, I'm homeward bound . . .

DAVID: Oh . . .

COSTOS: These boots are made for walking . . .

DAVID: Ohh . . .

COSTOS: Walk all over you.

DAVID: Yes.

COSTOS: I make you happy?

DAVID: Yes.

COSTOS: Very happy?

DAVID: Yes.

COSTOS: Sputnik. You go up like Sputnik. All the leaves are brown and the sky is grey . . .

DAVID: Yes.

COSTOS: I've been for a walk on a winter's day.

DAVID: Yes.

COSTOS: Sputnik. Into space.

DAVID: Ohh . . .

COSTOS: I'm not sleepy and there is no place I'm going to . . .

DAVID: Ohh . . .

COSTOS: If I didn't tell her, I could leave today . . .

DAVID: Ohhh.

COSTOS: California dreamin' on a winter's day . . .

DAVID: Ohhh!

[DAVID *has an orgasm.*]

[*Pause.*]

[COSTOS *sits up, startled.*]

COSTOS: So soon? Sputnik land so soon?

DAVID: I think so.

COSTOS: Too soon.

DAVID: I'm sorry.

COSTOS: I do not give pleasure?

DAVID: Yes. I'm sorry.

COSTOS: You do not like me?

DAVID: But I do.

COSTOS: Not very much.

DAVID: I do. Honestly. Very much. You give pleasure.

COSTOS: You make joke.

DAVID: No.

COSTOS: This truth?

DAVID: Yes. Truth.

COSTOS: Promise.

DAVID: Yes.

COSTOS: Great pleasure?

DAVID: Yes.
[*Pause.*]
Great.

COSTOS: I make you happy?

DAVID: Yes.
[*Pause.*]
Thank you.

COSTOS: Kiss me thank you.
[DAVID *kisses him.*]
Now I believe.

DAVID: Good.

COSTOS: Now give present.
[*He sits up.*]

DAVID: Oh. Really?

COSTOS: Yes.

DAVID: I must be dreaming.

COSTOS: No dream. Give present.

DAVID: You don't have to.
[*Pause.*]

COSTOS: Have to what?

DAVID: Give me a present. [*smiles*] You already did.

COSTOS: You make joke?

DAVID: No.

COSTOS: *You* give present.

DAVID: What?

COSTOS: You give present. To me.
[*Pause.*]

DAVID: Oh.

COSTOS: I close eyes.

[COSTOS *closes his eyes and holds out his hand.* DAVID *stares at him in silence.* COSTOS *opens his eyes.*]
Little present.
[*Pause.*]

DAVID: Why?

COSTOS: For pleasure.

DAVID: But I thought . . .

COSTOS: Because I give pleasure.

DAVID: I thought . . .

COSTOS: To say you like me.

DAVID: I thought . . . You found me . . .

COSTOS: To show I make you happy.

DAVID: I thought you thought I was . . . I thought you wanted to . . . I thought . . .
[*Pause.*]
I am stupid.

COSTOS: [*sings*] 'Cool down, evenin' in the city, Dressed so fine and a lookin' so pretty.'

DAVID: I was almost . . . someplace else. I am very stupid.

COSTOS: Watch.

DAVID: What?

COSTOS: Your watch.

DAVID: Yes?

COSTOS: Give me your watch.

DAVID: No.

COSTOS: Little present.

DAVID: Not my watch.

COSTOS: I like watch.

DAVID: It's *mine*.

COSTOS: I wear watch and think of you . . . underneath stars.

DAVID: No.

COSTOS: You buy another.

DAVID: Absolutely not.

COSTOS: Radio.

DAVID: I don't have one.

COSTOS: You must.

DAVID: I don't.

COSTOS: Americans have radios.

DAVID: I don't.

COSTOS: Listen to music.

DAVID: I don't.

COSTOS: Beatles.

DAVID: No radio.

COSTOS: Ring.

DAVID: No.

> [COSTOS *points to the ring on* DAVID's *finger.*]

COSTOS: This ring. Very nice.

DAVID: No.

COSTOS: Fit my finger.

> [*He pulls at the ring.*]

DAVID: No.

COSTOS: Same size.

DAVID: No.

COSTOS: Pretty ring . . .

DAVID: No. My grandmother gave it to me.

COSTOS: Grandmother?

DAVID: Yes. Old lady.

COSTOS: Oh.

> [*Pause.*]
>
> Very good. Very good. Grandmother. You keep.

DAVID: Thank you.

COSTOS: Camera.

DAVID: Certainly not.

COSTOS: Not big one. You have small one too.

DAVID: No. No cameras.

COSTOS: I go to room. Number six, I take camera. Small one.

DAVID: No.

COSTOS: Not big one.

DAVID: Neither one.

COSTOS: You don't like me.

DAVID: I do.

COSTOS: I do not give pleasure.

DAVID: You did.

COSTOS: You make fun of me.

DAVID: I don't.

COSTOS: You insult me.

DAVID: I'm not.

COSTOS: Then give me camera.

DAVID: I won't.

COSTOS: I lie on floor.

DAVID: No camera.

> [COSTOS *lies down on the ground.*]

COSTOS: I lie on floor. I scream. I say you hurt me.

DAVID: Hurt you?

COSTOS: [*holds his groin*] Here. In the sex. You do bad things to me. I can not move. I cry. You hurt me. I call the police.

DAVID: Police?

COSTOS: They come to room. Number six. They put you in prison. I am young. Seventeen. Against the law. I scream.

DAVID: No.

COSTOS: You hurt me. I can not move. I am screaming. [*shouts*] Police!

DAVID: Stop it.

COSTOS: You give me camera?

DAVID: No.

COSTOS: Police!

DAVID: You'll wake everybody up.

COSTOS: Police!

> [DAVID *puts his hand over* COSTOS' *mouth.* COSTOS *bites it.*]

DAVID: Ouch!

COSTOS: You touch me. You hurt me. You hurt my sex. Tomorrow King come. King find me. Under table. Almost dead. King take me in arms. King cry out — "My people, my people!" I screaming now. Police!

DAVID: You will wake the entire hotel.

COSTOS: I scream louder. Police!

DAVID: Alright! The watch! Take it!

> [DAVID *takes the watch off his wrist and holds it out.*]
>
> [*Pause.*]
>
> [COSTOS *sits up.*]

COSTOS: For me?

DAVID: Yes.

COSTOS: A present?

DAVID: Yes.

COSTOS: Your watch?

DAVID: Yes.

COSTOS: You sure?

DAVID: Yes.

COSTOS: You like me?

DAVID: Yes.

COSTOS: I make you happy?

DAVID: Yes.

[*Pause.*]

COSTOS: Very happy?

DAVID: Very happy.

COSTOS: Then I take it.

[*He grabs the watch.*]

What a surprise. A present!

[*He puts the watch on.*]

I am beautiful, no?

DAVID: No.

COSTOS: Thank you. I am beautiful. I have watch. I make you happy. You make me happy. I give you great pleasure. Now I go to sleep. You are nice. Pretty present. Pretty stars. Pretty night. [*sings*] 'We'll sing in the sunshine, We'll laugh everyday.'

[*He picks up his blanket.*]

[*sings*] 'We'll sing in the sunshine.'

[*He drapes the blanket on his shoulders.*]

[*sings*] 'And I'll be on my way.'

[COSTOS *leaves.*]

[DAVID *sits at a table. He leans back on his chair, closes his eyes, and begins to sing, in Hebrew.*]

DAVID: 'Ma nishtanah, halilah hazeh, mikahl halalos . . . '

[*The lights fade.*]

DAVID's *voice is heard.*

DAVID: [*voice only*] When I was a child, I sang it at Passover. 'Ma nishtanah . . . ' Why is this night different than any other? Why did that come racing into my head? Am I losing my mind? Michael!

[*Pause.*]

One thing washes over another. How long will it take for my hair to grow? Why do I sleep in my underwear? Cross this out. Don't write in this journal when you're drunk. Why is this night different? Because they talk to me now. Touch me. But it's still the same!

[*Pause.*]

If only my hair were long . . . if only something would change . . .

[*His voice fades away.*]

The lights rise.
The veranda. The next morning.
MRS. HONEY *is sitting at her table.*

MRS. HONEY: Waiting! I'm waiting. Hello! I'm waiting.
　　　　　　[*She rings her bell.*]
　　　　　　I demand my breakfast.
　　　　　　[*She rings the bell again.*]
　　　　　　[DAVID *enters. He goes to his table.*]
　　　　　　This is war, child. Good morning.
DAVID: Good morning.
MRS. HONEY: They have instituted a blockade of my table. They
　　　　　　have imposed sanctions. They are attempting to
　　　　　　terrorize my stomach. This inn offers room and
　　　　　　famine. Did you sleep well?
DAVID: No.
MRS. HONEY: Nor I. I anticipated trouble.
　　　　　　[*She rings the bell.*]
　　　　　　[*shouts*] I shall protest to the Ambassador!
　　　　　　[*Pause.*]
　　　　　　They shall not succeed. Mr. Gandhi, decent as
　　　　　　politicians go, often went without food, and *he*
　　　　　　became a country. I myself was such an atrocious
　　　　　　cook that I would spend days not touching a morsel.
　　　　　　The dentist, poor thing, and the children *had* to eat my
　　　　　　disastrous offerings — but I possessed the wisdom to
　　　　　　abstain. I believe your own religion has a day of ritual
　　　　　　starvation.
DAVID: Yom Kippur.
MRS. HONEY: Indeed. Then I hereby declare Yom Kippur at this
　　　　　　table.
DAVID: On Yom Kippur you atone for your sins.
MRS. HONEY: Fair enough — that will help me pass the time. My
　　　　　　primary sin was to book the wrong inn. But book I did,
　　　　　　and stay I shall. Nikos Kistos has joined battle with
　　　　　　the wrong pain in the neck.
　　　　　　[*Pause.*]
　　　　　　Did you hear noise last night? Screaming?
DAVID: No.
MRS. HONEY: In my mind, then. There was screaming in my mind.
　　　　　　[*She looks at* DAVID.]

	Do I spy a top button undone? And what is this late hour?
DAVID:	I overslept.
MRS. HONEY:	Did you?
DAVID:	Yes.
MRS. HONEY:	Glory be! Has retsina had a salutory effect? A little vice is not to be sneezed at.
DAVID:	What?
MRS. HONEY:	Too much wine is an excellent thing sometimes. After all, you need something to atone for on what is it called?
DAVID:	Yom Kippur.
MRS. HONEY:	"Dear God, I undid my button, forgive me." You're well on your way, boy, well on your way.
DAVID:	I'm hungry. I want my breakfast.
MRS. HONEY:	It is a pity you were not up slightly earlier, however. You might have witnessed a stupendous argument. The honeymoon couple. It seems she has misplaced her wedding ring and he is none too pleased about it. I had an enormous temptation to offer some solicitous advice and thus make things worse, but it's difficult to cause trouble on an empty stomach. And they did manage to wolf down their tea and toast, no matter how fierce their disagreement. I am not beyond stealing scraps.

[*She rings the bell.*]

If only this were louder. If it were not so heavy, I would travel with a gong.

[COSTOS *enters, humming 'What a Day for a Daydream'. He winks at* DAVID. DAVID *turns away.* MRS. HONEY *takes it in.* COSTOS *clears the dishes from a nearby table. He totally ignores* MRS. HONEY.]

I'm not going to say a word. I know he's going to ignore me. I have been sitting here for exactly one hour, screaming for service and ringing my bell, and he has paid me no mind. Do you like the way he looks? What do you think of his legs? Do you think he's ready to grow a beard yet?

[DAVID *shifts uneasily in his chair.*]

Have you noticed that he always hums? The dentist hummed, of course, but dentists are supposed to, so

they can drive their patients mad. On anyone else it is
most unattractive.

[NIKOS *enters, with his deck of cards.*]

NIKOS: Good morning, dear lady.

[*Pause.*]

MRS. HONEY: Well, well, well.

[NIKOS *sits at a table and starts to play solitaire.*]

NIKOS: Beautiful day.

MRS. HONEY: I suppose.

NIKOS: Not a cloud in the sky.

MRS. HONEY: No.

NIKOS: Good for the suntan.

MRS. HONEY: Excellent.

NIKOS: Have you enjoyed breakfast?

MRS. HONEY: Oh dear — how foolish of me. I forgot all about breakfast. I've been enjoying the view. Do you see that rock
jutting out into the sea? There's an old woman dressed
in black sitting on it. She has one eye. Most interesting.
I could watch her all day.

NIKOS: Would you like breakfast?

MRS. HONEY: Oh. I don't know.

NIKOS: We would be happy to serve you.

MRS. HONEY: Well, if it makes *you* happy, Nikos.

NIKOS: [*to* COSTOS] Ferte ris to ithico p roime.

COSTOS: Malista, kirie.

[*He goes into the kitchen.*]

MRS. HONEY: Well, well, well.

NIKOS: She has the evil eye.

MRS. HONEY: Who?

NIKOS: The woman on the rock.

MRS. HONEY: And it's her only one, what a pity.

[*Pause.*]

Is it aimed at you or me?

NIKOS: You look very pretty this morning, Mrs. Honey.

[*Pause.*]

MRS. HONEY: I loathe small talk. I practise it all the time, but I
loathe it in others. I smell deceit. I can taste it. You
won't get the table, Nikos.

NIKOS: I'm winning.

MRS. HONEY: What?

NIKOS: At cards.

[COSTOS *returns with a large tray containing two breakfasts.*

He lays a breakfast for DAVID — *orange juice, toast and tea.* MRS. HONEY *watches him with hungry eyes.* COSTOS *is humming 'Mr. Tambourine Man', making* DAVID *even more uncomfortable.* COSTOS *then brings his tray to* MRS. HONEY'S *table and gives her juice, tea and toast — and an extra plate, covered with a lid, which he lays down with a great flourish.*]

MRS. HONEY: Ah. This is sumptuous.

NIKOS: Of course.

MRS. HONEY: You seem to have given me something special.

NIKOS: Have we?

MRS. HONEY: Something not required. Something not on the menu. Something beyond orange juice, tea and toast.

NIKOS: A surprise, then.

MRS. HONEY: Indeed.

[*She stares at* NIKOS, *sizing up the situation.*]

Take it away.

NIKOS: Lift the lid.

MRS. HONEY: I don't want it. Take it away.

NIKOS: Lift the lid.

MRS. HONEY: I'm not hungry. Take it away.

NIKOS: Lift the lid.

MRS. HONEY: I think not. The specialty of the house is trouble. I smell deceit. Take it away.

[NIKOS *rises and goes to her table. He lifts the lid off of the plate. A jewel box lies underneath.*]

How on earth?

NIKOS: What is it?

MRS. HONEY: My jewel box.

NIKOS: Your jewel box, dear lady?

[MRS. HONEY *stares at him.*]

MRS. HONEY: Yes.

NIKOS: Astonishing.

MRS. HONEY: Where did you get my jewel box? Have you been rummaging through my room? I shall issue a complaint. I shall go to the police. This was packed away in a suitcase.

NIKOS: It is most attractive.

MRS. HONEY: Yes.

NIKOS: An antique.

MRS. HONEY: The dentist gave it to me. A long time ago. *What is it doing here?*

NIKOS: It is yours, though?

MRS. HONEY: You know it is.

NIKOS: Why don't you open it?

[*Pause.*]

MRS. HONEY: Ah.

[*Pause.*]

I think not.

NIKOS: Don't you want to make sure . . . ?

MRS. HONEY: Make sure?

NIKOS: That nothing is missing.

MRS. HONEY: No.

NIKOS: I think you must open it.

MRS. HONEY: I think I must not.

[NIKOS *flings the jewel box open.* MRS. HONEY *does not look at it.*]

Nothing is missing.

NIKOS: You haven't looked.

MRS. HONEY: No. I haven't.

[*She closes the box.* NIKOS *opens the box again.*]

NIKOS: Beautiful things.

MRS. HONEY: Yes.

NIKOS: Won't you look?

MRS. HONEY: No.

[NIKOS *removes a necklace from the box and holds it up.*]

NIKOS: This is lovely.

MRS. HONEY: My mother's.

[NIKOS *removes a bracelet and holds it up.*]

NIKOS: Exquisite.

MRS. HONEY: My mother's as well.

[NIKOS *holds up an earring.*]

NIKOS: And this?

MRS. HONEY: I bought it in New Delhi.

[NIKOS *holds up a ring.*]

NIKOS: And this?

MRS. HONEY: I don't know.

NIKOS: You don't know.

MRS. HONEY: I've never seen it before.

NIKOS: You've never seen it before?

MRS. HONEY: It's not mine.

NIKOS: It must be.

MRS. HONEY: It isn't. It's too vulgar. It's not mine.

NIKOS: Then whose is it?

MRS. HONEY: I have no idea.

NIKOS: And what is it doing in your jewel box?

MRS. HONEY: I have no idea.

NIKOS: Ah, but it could be . . . it looks remarkably like . . .

MRS. HONEY: Oh. I see. I see. Oh yes. I see.

NIKOS: The ring that until this morning adorned the finger of that sweet young girl on her honeymoon. She mislaid it.

MRS. HONEY: Indeed.

NIKOS: Is it hers?

MRS. HONEY: I would not know.

NIKOS: I think it is.

MRS. HONEY: It would not surprise me.
     [NIKOS *holds up a watch.*]

NIKOS: And what is this?

MRS. HONEY: A watch.

NIKOS: Yours?

MRS. HONEY: No.

NIKOS: Whose?

MRS. HONEY: I have no idea. I think this game is over.

NIKOS: Whose watch?

MRS. HONEY: I don't know. Nikos, leave it be.
     [NIKOS *turns to* DAVID.]

NIKOS: Is this your watch?

DAVID: Mine?

NIKOS: It looks like yours.

DAVID: No, it doesn't.

NIKOS: It looks like the watch I have noticed on your wrist.

DAVID: No.

NIKOS: Let me see your wrist.
     [*Silence.* DAVID *doesn't move.*]
     Please.
     [DAVID *holds out his wrist.*]
     No watch.

MRS. HONEY: Is it yours, child? Tell the truth.

DAVID: Yes. I think it is.

MRS. HONEY: How did it get here?

DAVID: I don't know.
     [MRS. HONEY *goes to* DAVID.]
     Listen to me, child, this is very important, this is crucial. Relatively few moments are crucial in life. This one is. Do you have any idea what happened to

your watch? Do you have any idea how your watch has come to be in my jewel box?

[DAVID *is silent.*]

Do you, child?

[*Silence.*]

DAVID: No.

MRS. HONEY: Then I'm lost.

[*She returns to her table.*]

Lost. [*to* NIKOS] And I suppose your cousin is the police chief?

NIKOS: No.

MRS. HONEY: Oh?

NIKOS: My uncle.

MRS. HONEY: [*smiles*] Of course.

NIKOS: I'd hate to disturb him.

[*Pause.*]

MRS. HONEY: You needn't. An Oxford education has served you well. You are clever, you and your brother. What have you done with him? Have you murdered him? There is, of course, no one to help me. I am totally unattached. The King must have his dinner. I believe there is a bus at noon. A local bus filled with livestock. Before I reclaim my jewel box please tell me if it contains any other surprises. Has the French scientist misplaced an ankle bracelet? And the Germans? Have they suffered a loss?

NIKOS: No. Just a ring and a watch.

MRS. HONEY: Well then . . .

[*She closes the jewel box.*]

Take the breakfast away, Nikos. I've lost my appetite. [*rises*] It *is* stupid. For a table! Good Lord.

[MRS. HONEY *leaves her table. She walks past* DAVID.]

DAVID: I'm sorry.

MRS. HONEY: It's not your fault. Don't worry. Others will talk to you. You'll see.

[*She starts to leave, then turns back.*]

I would like the photograph. Send it to me?

DAVID: Yes.

MRS. HONEY: Thank you.

DAVID: Where?

MRS. HONEY: Care of American Express.

DAVID: Which city?

MRS. HONEY: Choose one.

> [MRS. HONEY *leaves.*]

> [COSTOS *clears her table, humming. He looks over at* DAVID. DAVID *looks away.* NIKOS *is at his table again, playing solitaire.* DAVID *looks out to sea.*]

> [*The lights hold on them as we hear* DAVID's *voice.*]

DAVID: [*voice only*] There is a cool breeze tonight. From the Levant. And clouds. You cannot see the stars. You cannot see Albania. And it is raining. The afternoon was glorious, however. Very hot. I wasn't here when she took the bus. I was on the beach. The rain started around five. It's very light rain, more of a drizzle. The King cancelled his dinner. He didn't want to get wet.

> [COSTOS *continues to clean the table.*]

> [NIKOS *continues to play solitaire.*]

> [DAVID *continues to stare at the sea.*]

CURTAIN

PART TWO

Keeps Rainin'
all the Time

Santorini. Summer. 1990.

An enclosed veranda. There are beach chairs on the veranda as well as a wicker rocking chair. There is a door leading into the house and doors to a kitchen and a bathroom.

Behind this house, in the distance, a vista of Fira, the main village of Santorini: tiny whitewashed houses on tiny whitewashed streets, crisscrossing each other, built higher and higher on steep cliffs overlooking the sea.

It is raining, but still very warm.

Early morning.

DANIEL HOSANI *stands on the veranda, watching the rain. He is in his late forties. He is American, wasted-looking but oddly handsome. He wears shorts and an open shirt.*

OLIVER *enters. He is British, in his late forties.*

OLIVER: There you are, luv. It's five in the morning. I didn't hear you get up. What are you looking at? Rain. Nothing out there but rain. You can barely see the volcano. Silly life we lead, isn't it? Wake up every morning and stare at a dead crater in the middle of the sea. Still, we like it, don't we? Come on now, Mr. Hosani, let's sit down.

  [*He takes* DANIEL's *hand and leads him very gently to a chair.*]

That's a good boy. Aren't we a good boy? Down we
go . . .

[*He carefully places* DANIEL *in the chair.*]

You have some colour in your face. Yes, I like that, I
like that. It's the sleep. You slept thirty hours. Means
you're depressed, don't it, luv? Let's see . . .

[*He places his hand on* DANIEL's *wrist and takes an
acu-pulse.*]

Not bad, not bad . . .

[*He takes another pulse.*]

Ummm . . .

[*He takes another pulse.*]

Plenty to be depressed about. Another accident.
While you slept. A plant in France. Fire. Reactor still
burning. The air's filled with it. Coming this way. The
rain will bring it. What a way to start the nineties.

[*He takes another pulse.*]

Hmmm . . . liver's a little low. Hasn't stopped raining.
Used to freshen things, rain. Don't blame you sleeping,
luv. Your back's not too good — it's alright, we'll fix
it . . . Let's see — what else happened while you've
been asleep? Heather's come from New York. Dylan's
with her. And a Hollywood producer arrived last
night with a girlfriend. He wants to film your book. As
a *musical*. Oh, that's got the pulses racing!

DANIEL: Cream cheese.

OLIVER: Exactly.

[DANIEL *pulls away from* OLIVER.]

DANIEL: Beautiful.

OLIVER: What?

DANIEL: The apricot is beautiful.

OLIVER: Well, yes, always has been.

DANIEL: Don't discover me.

OLIVER: I don't think I can.

DANIEL: Please.

OLIVER: Don't worry.

DANIEL: Tangerine.

OLIVER: Don't know tangerine.

DANIEL: Tangerine!

[*He sits on the edge of the chair.*]

OLIVER: Why are you getting so excited? Come on . . . let's be
a good boy . . . let's calm down . . .

DANIEL: I want to gallop.

OLIVER: It's better if you don't talk, Mr. Hosani. You know that.

DANIEL: Do you adagio?

OLIVER: No.

[DANIEL *stands up.*]

DANIEL: It's a nomad. Over there. Nomad! Splendour! Steal it. Mama!

[*He walks forward.*]

OLIVER: You can't walk outside. It's raining.

DANIEL: Tangerine.

OLIVER: I don't know tangerine. Come on, down we go . . .

[*He places him back into the chair.*]

That's right . . . that's a good boy . . . there's nothing outside . . .

DANIEL: If . . . if . . .

OLIVER: Yes, yes . . .

DANIEL: If I could lambchop.

OLIVER: If only we could all lambchop.

DANIEL: I want to . . .

OLIVER: Well you can't, not today . . . let's just lie back . . . that's better, isn't it? . . . don't we feel better now? . . . nice and quiet . . . let's be very calm . . .

[*He goes to the table and removes a tray filled with needles.*]

DANIEL: Starlight.

OLIVER: There. Calm.

[*He takes an acupunture needle and sticks it into* DANIEL's *forehead.*]

Like a good boy.

DANIEL: Starlight.

[OLIVER *puts a needle into* DANIEL's *hand.*]

OLIVER: Yes, luv, starlight.

[*Pause.*]

Whatever that is.

[*Blackout.*]

Church bells ring — many kinds of church bells.

The lights rise. Three hours later.

HEATHER *is in the rocking chair. She is in her late forties, American, and wears a light caftan. She is smoking a cigarette. A map lies on her lap.*

DANIEL *is on the beach chair next to her, staring straight ahead. The needles have been removed.*

HEATHER: I guess volcanoes are classic manic-depressives.
Don't you think? Danny? It's so calm, it's been calm
for thousands of years, but once that piece of rock out
there was the life of the party.

 [*Pause.*]

Oh shit, Danny.

 [*Pause.*]

It's not supposed to rain like this. The weather has
altered, you know. Summer is no longer summer, dry
is no longer dry. The planet's distressed. I couldn't
see the stars last night. Do you realize they are exactly
the same stars that you and I stared at in Corfu? It
doesn't seem that long ago. We were so young. Now
look at us, eh? But *they* haven't changed. Danny?

 [*Pause.*]

Oh shit, Danny.

 [*Pause.*]

You know, you've grown handsome. There's some
kind of irony in that. Your looks have improved with
age. You were so awkward then. At least that part of
the book is true. Danny?

 [*Pause.*]

My son is going to kill himself and he doesn't even
know it. What am I going to do?

 [*Pause.*]

You used to have so much to say.

 [*Pause.*]

I have no pity for you.

 [*Pause.*]

Oh shit, Danny.

 [*Pause.*]

[*calls into the kitchen*] Oliver — what are you doing?

OLIVER: [*off*] Be right there.

HEATHER: I'll bet the tourists have fled. What's a Greek island
without sun? Don't the church bells ever stop ringing?
We're on the edge of a cliff. This whole town is on the
edge of a cliff. That's not reassuring.

 [*Pause.*]

Is it?

 [OLIVER *enters with a tray.*]

OLIVER: Coffee?

HEATHER: No thanks.

OLIVER: Wake you up.

HEATHER: He won't talk.
          [OLIVER *gives* DANIEL *a cup of coffee.*]
OLIVER: Sometimes he does. Sometimes he doesn't.
HEATHER: Where's Dylan?
OLIVER: Still sleeping.
HEATHER: Why isn't he up?
OLIVER: Drink some coffee.
HEATHER: Take it away. Caffeine's dangerous. I can show him this map. I have a plan. He'll think I'm crazy, though. He always does. Where's whats-his-name from Hollywood — Barnaby Grace?
OLIVER: Sleeping.
HEATHER: Everyone's sleeping.
          [*She starts to cough, then wheeze, then can't catch her breath.*]
OLIVER: Are you alright?
          [HEATHER*'s breath comes back; she stops coughing.* OLIVER *places his hand on her wrists and takes her pulse.*]
HEATHER: No. Don't.
          [*She pulls her wrist away.*]
          You'll be alarmed. I don't want your needles. I'm in remission, anyway. Everything's alright.
OLIVER: Why are you smoking?
HEATHER: I can't stop. I tried. You put needles in my ear once, remember? Ha! Didn't help. Well — we all have at least one passion that's killing us. The joke is my lungs are fine. It's everything else that's shot.
          [*Pause.*]
          Hey, Danny, I'm dying. Did you know that?
          [*Pause.*]
          You could address that point at least, you bastard.
          [*Pause.*]
          What is he thinking of? When he dreams, does he hear the right words? Does he ever make himself laugh?
          [*Pause.*]
          This house was a good idea. At least he's someplace beautiful — and reasonably bizarre. That's important for him. Did you know they call Santorini the island of vampires? Is that it, Danny, is that what you've become? Then if only you'd *bite*.
          [*Pause.*]
          Hey, Danny, remember — [*sings*] 'We'll sing in the sunshine, We'll laugh everyday.'

[*Pause.*]
The voice is gone, eh? I thought the part of the brain that receives music is self-contained. Is it, Oliver?

OLIVER: Seems to be.

HEATHER: Guess my singing no longer qualifies as music. No more two-bit career. Well, folksongs are out of date anyhow, aren't they?
[*Pause.*]
Will you play tapes for him?

OLIVER: Soon.

HEATHER: You're so wise. Where the hell is Dylan? Do you know he's leaving for Paris in the morning?

OLIVER: Yes.

HEATHER: He's killing himself.

OLIVER: Do you want some tea?

HEATHER: Can't you sneak a needle into Dylan and knock him out for a week?

OLIVER: Do you want some orange juice?

HEATHER: Maybe. Where are the oranges from? What kind of soil do they grow in?

OLIVER: Oranges grow on trees.

HEATHER: [*laughs*] Oh, Oliver, thank God you're here.

OLIVER: I get paid well.

HEATHER: I know. I sign the cheques. Do you ever give yourself needles?

OLIVER: Have done.

HEATHER: Could you kill yourself?

OLIVER: With a needle?

HEATHER: Yes.

OLIVER: I suppose.

HEATHER: Painless?

OLIVER: Quite.

HEATHER: Lucky you.
[DYLAN *enters. He is nineteen. He is wearing a bathing suit and has a Walkman plugged into his ear.*]

DYLAN: Morning, guys.

HEATHER: Where are you going?
[DYLAN *doesn't hear.*]
Dylan!

DYLAN: Huh?
[HEATHER *motions towards the tape-machine.*]

HEATHER: Turn it down.
[DYLAN *turns the volume down.*]

DYLAN: What?
HEATHER: Where are you going?
DYLAN: Swimming.
HEATHER: In the *rain*?
DYLAN: Yup.
HEATHER: You'll catch cold.
DYLAN: I'm going to, like, get wet either way. Wet's wet.
          [*He starts for the door.*]
HEATHER: Dylan?
DYLAN: Now what?
HEATHER: Have you reconsidered your plans?
DYLAN: Nope.
HEATHER: Don't go to Paris.
DYLAN: Oh, Mom, give it a rest, will you?
HEATHER: There's a cloud heading for Paris . . .
          [DYLAN *turns the volume up.*]
DYLAN: Can't hear you.
          [HEATHER *rises.*]
HEATHER: Filled with radioactive fallout.
          [*She pulls the plug out of his ear.*]
DYLAN: Ouch! You're being, like, very sixties.
HEATHER: This is real.
DYLAN: Mom, everything is real. If I dealt with real I wouldn't
          deal.
HEATHER: *What?*
DYLAN: Your radioactive cloud is hoppin' around. It's, like,
          on a jag. It's a regular tourist bus. If it's Tuesday,
          like, it must be Venice, you know? It's coming to
          Greece too. And Tokyo, New York, Moscow, all them
          places . . . Like, where do you want me to go, Mars?
HEATHER: Sumba.
DYLAN: What?
HEATHER: It was just a thought.
DYLAN: Is this one of those days when you're out to lunch?
HEATHER: I was just thinking about Sumba.
DYLAN: I'm, like, afraid to ask — but — what's Sumba?
HEATHER: An island. Near Sumbawa.
DYLAN: Oh, of course. I should have known.
          [*He pats her on the head.*]
          I'm goin' swimming.
          [HEATHER *sits on the floor and spreads out her map.*]
HEATHER: Look — I'll show you.
DYLAN: I don't believe this. Maps!

HEATHER: [*tracing a path on the map*] Here . . . this is Java . . .

DYLAN: Who would believe this?

HEATHER: And Java is not far from Sumbawa . . .

DYLAN: I'm like, not telling this to my friends, no way — they think you're weird enough . . .

HEATHER: You're not looking!

[DYLAN *sits next to her.*]

DYLAN: Mom, this ain't good for you.

HEATHER: Alright, it is a bit unusual, but don't reject it without some thought. I do have my own logic. I phoned Fred last night, in New York. Remember Fred, the television weather-man?

DYLAN: No. Did you ask him when the rain's gonna stop?

HEATHER: He knows about prevailing winds.

DYLAN: Oliver, please, give her a needle.

HEATHER: He says no place is totally safe . . .

DYLAN: This is loony tunes.

HEATHER: But as far as he can tell, the *safest* spot is just about here . . .

[*She points to a place on the map.*]

DYLAN: Where?

HEATHER: Here.

DYLAN: Sumba?

HEATHER: Yes.

DYLAN: It's in the middle of nowhere.

HEATHER: Exactly.

DYLAN: A couple of banana trees and some sand.

HEATHER: Probably.

DYLAN: I'll bet you're serious about this.

HEATHER: I'll give you the money. I'll even go with you.

DYLAN: To Sumba?

HEATHER: Yes.

DYLAN: Do they have daily flights from Santorini?

HEATHER: This is *serious.*

DYLAN: Mom, you're goin' round the bend. This kind of obsession with nuclear disaster has made you positively ga-ga. You, like, really want me to parachute into the South Pacific?

HEATHER: It's a bit fanciful, I suppose. Alright — let's compromise. Forget Sumba. Stay here.

DYLAN: I'm goin' to Paris. And I'm goin' for a swim. And they both ain't gonna kill me.

HEATHER: Dylan, the accident was yesterday. The cloud is at its fiercest now. Paris will get the worst of it.

DYLAN: So I'll glow slightly more than usual. Mom, this is, like, the third accident in two years. We've all fried our insides already, you know? It doesn't matter if I go to Paris. And if I do go to Paris, I can sell my language computer and if I sell my language computer, I can make, like, maybe half a million bucks and then possibly I can, like, be free to radiate on a slightly more mellow plane. You know what I mean, huh?

HEATHER: You're just a kid. What do you care about half a million dollars?

DYLAN: Oh, play that back — just play that one back. You know, you should be proud of me. I ain't a junkie, like everyone else. I am, technically, like, a genius.

HEATHER: You have no passion.

DYLAN: Passion sucks.

[*He points to* DANIEL.]

Look at him. That's passion. Look at you, eating yourself up all your life because the world is wrong. So, hey, Mom, it *is* wrong, it *is* unfair, it *is* galloping down the drain — so what else is new? What the hell can you do about it? You're killing yourself, like, quicker than any bomb would. You've got major fallout inside of you. You're supposed to take it easy. You're all tensed up. Why don't you exercise?

HEATHER: I'll be tranquil — absolutely tranquil — if you stay away from Paris.

DYLAN: Fuck off, O.K.? — just fuck off — I won't take the blame for your insides. I don't take the blame for nothin'.

[ALIKI *enters. She is in her mid-twenties and very beautiful. She wears a bikini and has a Walkman plugged into her ear.*]

ALIKI: Good morning.

OLIVER: Morning.

[ALIKI *walks outside.* DYLAN *stares after her.*]

DYLAN: Who is *she*?

OLIVER: The producer's companion. Name's Aliki. Greek. A student. She picked him up in an Athens bar.

[HEATHER *and* DYLAN *look at* OLIVER, *amazed.*]

I asked.

DYLAN: Shit.

[*He goes to the door.*]

I don't totally lack passion.

[*He follows* ALIKI *outside, turning the volume up on his Walkman.*]

HEATHER: [*shouts after him*] That's not passion.

[*She starts to cough and gasp.*]

Damn it . . .

[OLIVER *goes to her.*]

No, Oliver, I'm O.K.

OLIVER: You're not, luv.

HEATHER: I am. I can't catch my breath. I'm O.K. Leave me alone.

[*She stops gasping — breathes easier.*]

Where the hell is Barnaby Grace? We have to discuss that film. See? I'm alright now. Maybe I should phone someone. But who? Fred, the weatherman? Dylan won't believe him. His father's dead. There's only me.

[OLIVER *seats her in a chair and massages her neck.*]

Alright, you can do that . . . He's invented a computer that stores twenty thousand words in twelve languages. Isn't it amazing? And the kid can't even speak *English*. Oh, Oliver, your hands, your hands . . . Did you know that Danny's parents tore their clothing into shreds and fasted for twenty-four hours when his book came out? They disowned him. Their son was dead. I thought it totally inhuman then. Now I envy their skill. What kind of mother am I if I don't know how to make my son feel guilty? Ohh . . . your hands . . .

OLIVER: I want you to relax.

[HEATHER *pulls away from him.*]

HEATHER: No — no. I don't have time. Why don't you put on his tapes? Go. Go!

[OLIVER *stares at her, then walks away. He picks up a Walkman on the table and places a cassette in it. He goes to* DANIEL *and gently helps him to rise and move to another chair on the other side of the veranda.*]

OLIVER: Come on, luv, time for some music. Your guardian doesn't want to relax. She's not smart, not like you.

HEATHER: The world is burning — how the hell can I *relax*?

[*She sits on the floor next to the map.*]

What does it take to make a wind shift?

OLIVER: These are all Greek folk melodies. We like them, don't we? That's my boy.

[OLIVER *places the earphones on* DANIEL *and turns the Walkman on.*]

[DANIEL *smiles.*]

[OLIVER *moves away.*]

The music sounds slightly Hebraic. That's why he responds.

HEATHER: Remember the days when people listened to music *together*?

[BARNABY GRACE *enters. He is American, in his late twenties.*]

BARNABY: Morning.

HEATHER: Ah. Mr. Grace.

BARNABY: [*looking over at* DANIEL] Is that really him?

HEATHER: More or less.

BARNABY: Daniel Hosani. It's hard to take in.

HEATHER: Take it in.

BARNABY: It's a real believe-it-or-noter, isn't it?

HEATHER: Pardon?

BARNABY: I thought he was dead.

HEATHER: Not quite.

BARNABY: I can't believe it's him.

HEATHER: It's him.

BARNABY: He's in a living-sad situation, eh?

HEATHER: Pardon?

BARNABY: Had some kind of stroke?

HEATHER: Oh. Yes.

BARNABY: When?

HEATHER: Three years ago.

BARNABY: Wow. He must be slow-timing it now.
[*Pause.*]
I can't believe it's him.

HEATHER: You said that.

BARNABY: Daniel Hosani.

OLIVER: Would you like some coffee, Mr. Grace?

BARNABY: Yes — please — if it's a sugarless situation.
[OLIVER *goes into the kitchen.*]

HEATHER: Coffee isn't healthy.

BARNABY: I'm sorry if I was strange when we arrived last evening.

HEATHER: Strange?

BARNABY: Incoherent.

HEATHER: Oh. It's alright. Don't worry. You're incoherent this morning as well.

BARNABY: I was exhausted. All those steps.

HEATHER: From the harbour?

BARNABY: Yes. We climbed up eight hundred of them to get

	here. I counted. A real grow-tired experience. Is this island really made of lava?
HEATHER:	Some of it.
BARNABY:	No wonder it's such a look-strange place.
	[*Pause.*]
	Daniel Hosani.
HEATHER:	Yes — that's very good — that's his name. Now why don't we discuss the film you plan to make?
BARNABY:	I can't believe it's him. I admire him so much. What a feel-good writer. I was only fifteen when I read the book. But I understood every word.
HEATHER:	Ah.
BARNABY:	It made me glad to be alive, even though it had its depressing moments.
HEATHER:	Ah.
	[OLIVER *arrives with some coffee.*]
BARNABY:	It had a real smile-on-face tang with a slight seem-sad taste.
	[HEATHER *pulls* OLIVER *aside.*]
HEATHER:	Oliver — I've just had a blinding flash. My species is extinct.
BARNABY:	It's still a favourite of mine.
	[OLIVER *hands him the coffee.*]
	Thank you. I listen to it often.
HEATHER:	Listen?
BARNABY:	Books-on-tape.
HEATHER:	Oh yes.
BARNABY:	You can listen while you work.
HEATHER:	Yes.
BARNABY:	I haven't *read* a book in years.
HEATHER:	Well, well, well.
BARNABY:	She says that all the time.
HEATHER:	Who?
BARNABY:	Mrs. Honey.
HEATHER:	Oh.
	[*Pause.*]
	He picked it up from me.
	[DANIEL *begins to hum a tune, a Greek melody.*]
	Listen!
OLIVER:	He remembers melodies.
HEATHER:	I used to know this song . . .
	[*She begins to hum.*]
OLIVER:	Sometimes he'll sing a word or two in Greek.

BARNABY: [*to* OLIVER] Am I correct in assuming he is now a thinking-impaired citizen?

OLIVER: Excuse me?

BARNABY: His mind is disabled.

OLIVER: His mind is fine.

HEATHER: You don't know anything about air currents, do you, Mr. Grace?

BARNABY: I've come here to make a pitch.

HEATHER: Yes, yes.

BARNABY: But how can I throw my concepts to a brain-scramble?

HEATHER: You throw them to *me*. I'm his legal guardian, God help me. Well, there was no one else. His parents no longer acknowledged him. His book was too openly gay. I'm his oldest friend, maybe his only friend. I was even with him that summer.

BARNABY: You were *there*?

HEATHER: Yes.

BARNABY: But you're not in the book.

HEATHER: Who says the book is true?

BARNABY: It has to be.

HEATHER: It's writing.

BARNABY: It's filled with truth.

HEATHER: That's different.

BARNABY: I can't believe it . . . I can't believe you were actually there . . . I can't believe he's actually Daniel Hosani . . . I can't believe what's happened to him.

HEATHER: Why not? What's happened to him is completely unoriginal. I have no pity for him. None. Damn him! You can't imagine that's Daniel Hosani? Big fucking deal, who was Daniel Hosani anyhow? A yo-yo, an American yo-yo. Do you know what I mean? Up and down. Famous too soon, thrown aside too quick. It's too boring. It happens to almost everyone. Do you understand? He was dispensable. Disposable. He was waste. You've probably produced four bad movies with his story in it. A kid writes a book. The critics say he's the new Fitzgerald. It sells a million copies. He's all over television. Magazine covers. Fashion layouts . . . He's happy. He drinks, he snorts, he fucks. He has a wonderful time. He's famous. But he can't write any more. So he gets depressed. He goes away. He becomes a Buddhist. Then he does write again. About being famous. His second book. The critics say he's lost his innocence. The public isn't interested any more. He's depressed again. He travels again. He becomes a Catholic. Lovers come and go. He is not really very nice. And then the royal mile — Alcohol. Cocaine. Heroin. Car crashes. Hospitals. Shock treatment. Stroke. It's the same old story. Now he can't find the right words. It's a form of aphasia. What did it, the stroke, the shock treatment, the drugs? Who knows? His mind substitutes. He will, for instance, say olive tree instead of automobile. Sometimes he says the right word. There's no pattern. He makes sense and he doesn't. His brain's gone and it's not. He's alive and he's dead. What more do you have to know?

[DANIEL *stops humming.*]

Look — time is running out fast. I wanted to lay eyes on you. I have. Good. Now I want to hear your ideas. I even want Danny to hear them. Your offer is financially not unattractive. So talk to us. How do you plan to make this movie? How can you turn Danny's book into a *musical?*

BARNABY: I have a vision about this. Daniel Hosani wrote a people-story and we should return to people-stories in Hollywood and people-stories should sing. I have the studios with me in this, and much of the industry, and most importantly, Jesus.

HEATHER: Pardon?

BARNABY: Jesus.

HEATHER: Oh.

BARNABY: You see, I was lost myself, very lost, and then I found Him. A light-blinder, alright. Now I think of Jesus as my co-producer. We're incorporated, if you know what I mean. He turned me away from gadgets and back to humanity. You see, we've spent years making look-smart films about — say — a boy and his pet monkey and his spaceship and we got carried away with that spaceship and all the special effects it entailed. Jesus has taken me away from space. He hit me with a down-to-earther. Now I want to concentrate on the boy and the monkey. And I want to know, I really want to know, what makes that monkey tick.

[*Pause.*]

HEATHER: Ah.

BARNABY: Look, I have things with me — notes, charts, tapes, outlines — let me show you . . .

HEATHER: I really want Danny to hear this.

BARNABY: Good. I'll get them.

[BARNABY *leaves.*]

HEATHER: Oh my God, Oliver, he's twelve years old, he has the brain of a lemon, he talks in tongues and he thinks the book is about some fucking monkey!

OLIVER: Won't this upset Mr. Hosani?

HEATHER: I hope so.

OLIVER: You're up to something.

HEATHER: Maybe.

OLIVER: You're totally unfocused.

HEATHER: I know.

OLIVER: Let me help.

HEATHER: No. Leave me alone. Don't help me. There is no time.

[DYLAN *and* ALIKI *run in from the pool. They are both wet.* ALIKI *still has her Walkman plugged in.*]

DYLAN: Towels! Help! Oliver! Towels!

OLIVER: He thinks I'm the maid.

[*He goes into the bathroom.*]

[ALIKI *is dancing to the beat of her music.* DYLAN *puts his wet hands on her back.*]

ALIKI: Don't.

DYLAN: Why not?

ALIKI: Hands — freezing.

[DYLAN *goes to* HEATHER.]

DYLAN: She's, like, bored to death with that producer. Maybe I can lure her to Paris. What do you think, Mom?

HEATHER: I think you should stay here.

DYLAN: Listen, drop the red alert for a sec, O.K.? Forget nuclear and think sex — do you like her?

HEATHER: Does my opinion matter?

DYLAN: Of course not.

[OLIVER *returns from the bathroom with two large bathtowels. He gives one to* ALIKI *and throws one to* DYLAN.]

OLIVER: You're welcome.

DYLAN: [*to* ALIKI] Can I, like, dry you?

ALIKI: What?

DYLAN: [*shouts*] Can I, like, dry you?

ALIKI: No.

DYLAN: You can dry me.

ALIKI: What?

DYLAN: Dry me.

ALIKI: Dry yourself.

DYLAN: Do you wanna go to Paris?

ALIKI: No.

DYLAN: Do you wanna kiss?

ALIKI: No.

DYLAN: Do you wanna see my computer?

ALIKI: [*laughs*] No.

DYLAN: Ah, shit, come to Paris. Fly with me to Athens, like, this afternoon, and then Paris tomorrow.

  [ALIKI *removes her earphones.*]

ALIKI: This afternoon? Athens?

DYLAN: Yes.

ALIKI: Three-o-clock flight?

DYLAN: Yes.

ALIKI: We were supposed to take this plane. But this Jesus Man change plans. Now we take boat to Crete.

DYLAN: Like, forget him. Come with me.

ALIKI: You very sure? Three-o-clock?

DYLAN: Yes.

HEATHER: Dylan? Are you going to shower?

DYLAN: Mom — not now. I'm seducing.

HEATHER: Take a shower.

DYLAN: I'm already wet.

HEATHER: From the rain. You don't know what's coming down in the rain. There's still some fallout around from this winter's accident.

DYLAN: Oh, put a lid on it.

ALIKI: She is very right. Take shower.

DYLAN: Yes?

ALIKI: I think so.

DYLAN: You do?

ALIKI: Listen to the mother.

  [DYLAN *looks at* ALIKI, *then* HEATHER.]

DYLAN: Beats me.

  [*He goes to the bathroom door.*]

  O.K. I take shower.

  [*He enters the bathroom.*]

  [*Pause.*]

ALIKI: I take shower too.

  [*She goes into the bathroom.*]

  [*Pause.*]

DYLAN: [*off*] Jesus!

HEATHER: Jesus seems to be on everyone's lips today.
          [*Pause.*]
          Oliver?
OLIVER: What?
HEATHER: Did that just happen?
OLIVER: Suppose so.
HEATHER: She's in the shower with my son?
OLIVER: Suppose so.
HEATHER: Oh.
          [*Pause.*]
          Have they been introduced?
          [*Pause.*]
          Well.
          [*Pause.*]
          Well . . .
          [*Pause.*]
          What do you think they're doing?
          [OLIVER *removes the headphones from* DANIEL.]
OLIVER: Here, let's have that now, Mr. Hosani. No more
          music. That's right, that's a good boy. Do we want to
          take a walk around the house?
          [DANIEL *shakes his head 'no'.*]
          Alright, let's just sit here then.
          [DANIEL *brushes* OLIVER *aside with his hands.*]
          Alright, luv, I'll leave you alone.
HEATHER: Do you think they're washing each other?
OLIVER: Probably.
HEATHER: That's nice.
          [*Pause.*]
          That's very clean.
          [*Pause.*]
          Did they lock the door?
OLIVER: Didn't hear the latch.
HEATHER: Ah.
          [*Pause.*]
          It's unlocked, then?
OLIVER: Yes.
          [*Pause.*]
HEATHER: Still raining outside?
OLIVER: Yes.
HEATHER: Shame.
OLIVER: Yes.
HEATHER: Rain.

[*A long pause.*]

[*Suddenly both* HEATHER *and* OLIVER *sprint to the door of the bathroom. They stand at the door, listening.*]

This is awful.

OLIVER: I know.

HEATHER: Completely immature.

OLIVER: I know.

HEATHER: We shouldn't be doing this.

OLIVER: I know.

HEATHER: What do you hear?

OLIVER: Water.

HEATHER: What else?

OLIVER: Just water.

HEATHER: Look through the keyhole.

OLIVER: Absolutely not.

HEATHER: Go on.

OLIVER: I've never done anything like that in my life.

HEATHER: Just a peek.

OLIVER: No.

[HEATHER *laughs and tickles him.*]

HEATHER: A tiny peek.

OLIVER: It's good to see you smile.

HEATHER: Go on.

OLIVER: Alright.

[*He gets down on his knees and peeks through the keyhole.*]

HEATHER: Well?

OLIVER: Steam. I see steam.

HEATHER: And?

OLIVER: More steam.

[*He rises from his knees.*]

HEATHER: Then open the door.

OLIVER: *What?*

HEATHER: Just a crack.

OLIVER: You open the door.

HEATHER: Don't you fancy him?

OLIVER: Of course not.

HEATHER: Really?

OLIVER: Well. A little.

HEATHER: So open the door.

OLIVER: You open it. Do *you* fancy him?

HEATHER: He's my son!

OLIVER: So?

HEATHER: Well — I fancy him the way mothers do.

[*Pause.*]
Which is probably more than you think.
[*Pause.*]
But not quite enough for alarm. I do like the way he looks naked. Like his father. Open the door. It has to be you. I've always given him independence. I mustn't intrude. But you can. Go on, go on . . .

OLIVER: It's against everything I believe in.
HEATHER: I know. Go on.
[*Pause.*]
OLIVER: This is awful.
[*Pause.*]

[OLIVER *quietly opens the door, just a crack. He looks in.*]
HEATHER: Well?
OLIVER: Umm . . .
HEATHER: Yes?
OLIVER: Ummm . . .
HEATHER: What's ummmm?
OLIVER: Nice.
HEATHER: Nice?
OLIVER: Very nice.
HEATHER: What are they doing?
OLIVER: Umm . . .
HEATHER: Oliver!
OLIVER: Ummm . . . ummm . . .
HEATHER: Oh shit.
[*She pushes* OLIVER *aside and looks through the crack.*]
Oh. Ah.
[*Pause.*]
Ummm . . .
[*Pause.*]
Nice.
[*She closes the door.*]
It's sweet. It's so sweet. Isn't it sweet?
OLIVER: Yes.
HEATHER: Rubbing soap over each other.
OLIVER: Yes.
HEATHER: Feeling each other.
OLIVER: Yes.
HEATHER: That's very sweet.
OLIVER: Yes.
[OLIVER *opens the door again and looks, then closes the door.*]

HEATHER: What are they doing now?

OLIVER: Soap — still.

HEATHER: Oh Oliver — remember pleasure?

OLIVER: Barely.

HEATHER: Losing yourself.

OLIVER: Not really.

HEATHER: There *were* times, weren't there?

OLIVER: Few.

HEATHER: Do you have lovers?

OLIVER: People find me comforting and wise, two qualities that totally negate sex-appeal. That's the truth, luv. I know how to make people feel better, genuinely feel better, and it has nothing to do with stroking a nipple. If I say I want that, they think I've betrayed their trust. The last time was five years ago.

HEATHER: My God!

OLIVER: And he didn't speak English. He had no idea I could soothe.

HEATHER: Don't you miss it?

OLIVER: All the time.

HEATHER: That's what I hated most about the hospital. My luck — the doctors were all young and handsome. They would lean over me and breathe on me and smile and touch me and I felt so humiliated — all those tubes up my nose and scars down my body. I wanted to feel something or even to think something sexual, and I couldn't.

OLIVER: Just as well, luv. Sex is too dangerous now.

HEATHER: That's not true. You can do it — but safely.
[*Pause.*]
My God, do you think they're being cautious? What are they doing?

OLIVER: [*peeking through the door*] Soap.

HEATHER: That's a lot of soap. Dylan isn't cautious. If he was, he wouldn't go to Paris. For Christ's sake, Oliver, we have to get them out of there.

OLIVER: You're off again.

HEATHER: Do you have a condom?

OLIVER: What?

HEATHER: Slip a condom under the door!

OLIVER: [*laughs*] Heather . . .

HEATHER: It isn't funny. I'm deadly serious. Slip a fucking condom under the door. Stop laughing. I don't want him to die. The world is burning, Oliver.

OLIVER: Stop it.

[*He grabs her by the neck and steadies her.*]

[BARNABY *enters carrying a pile of notes.*]

BARNABY: I'm ready. I have everything. Except my companion. A real look-pretty, but I've misplaced her. She attached herself to me in Athens, you know. I don't want you to think . . .

HEATHER: You needn't explain. She's swimming.

BARNABY: In the rain?

HEATHER: Yes. I am curious, I must admit — how do you square her with Jesus?

BARNABY: He's very flexible about my personal life.

HEATHER: Ah.

BARNABY: You know, I still can't believe that you were there.

HEATHER: Where?

BARNABY: Corfu.

HEATHER: Oh. Oh yes.

[OLIVER *takes* HEATHER *aside and whispers to her.*]

OLIVER: Shower's stopped.

HEATHER: Good.

OLIVER: Not good. Coming out.

HEATHER: Oh shit. What do we do?

OLIVER: Divert.

[OLIVER *returns to the bathroom door.* HEATHER *takes* BARNABY*'s arm and leads him away.*]

HEATHER: Yes — I was with him all summer.

OLIVER: And Mrs. Honey?

HEATHER: Yes.

[*The bathroom door starts to open.* OLIVER *leans against it and closes it. The door pushes him forward; he pushes it back.*]

BARNABY: What was her actuality factor?

HEATHER: Pardon?

BARNABY: Was she real?

HEATHER: Sure. By and large. Basically. There was a woman named Foster.

[*She manoeuvres* BARNABY *into a chair, facing the sea.*]

BARNABY: And the table?

HEATHER: Yes. I suppose. Fairly true.

BARNABY: And they made her leave?

HEATHER: In a way.

[OLIVER *lets the bathroom door open. He motions* ALIKI *out onto the veranda. She sees* BARNABY *and slips quietly off.*]

BARNABY: They found the watch on her?

HEATHER: Oh yes.

BARNABY: Amazing.

HEATHER: But then she was a kleptomaniac.

BARNABY: Oh. And David?

HEATHER: Well, Daniel was *there*. But then so was I. He certainly wasn't travelling alone.

BARNABY: And the waiter seduced him?

HEATHER: Probably the other way round.

[OLIVER *motions* DYLAN *onto the veranda.* DYLAN *quietly sneaks off.*]

BARNABY: Oh. And poor Mrs. Honey just kept on travelling?

HEATHER: Yes. But he left the reason out.

BARNABY: The reason?

HEATHER: Actually, the reason for the dentist's death.

BARNABY: The dentist?

HEATHER: Her husband, remember?

BARNABY: Oh, of course, but he's offscreen.

HEATHER: Indeed. Danny failed to say that the dentist's cancer was caused by radiation. That little desert place in Utah was known as a downwind town. Do you know what that is?

BARNABY: No.

HEATHER: Downwind from Nevada, from the atomic testing site. They had been exposed to radiation for years. No one ever told them to take precautions. Out of fifty families in that desert town only three escaped cancer. Mrs. Foster was too bright by half — she figured it out by the time the dentist died, but no one would listen to her, certainly not the government who actively denied it until a few years ago, and not her children, who were in great danger themselves. They told her to shut up, the way Dylan tells me to shut up. She was consumed by blinding sanity. Which made her rather a leper. She was never good company. So she took off — for everyplace else. He left all of that out.

[*Pause.*]

BARNABY: That isn't something we can use.

HEATHER: Use?

BARNABY: In the movie.

HEATHER: Guess not.

BARNABY: Jesus doesn't disapprove of nuking, you know.

HEATHER: Oh?

BARNABY: In its place.
        [*Pause.*]

HEATHER: Oh — *that* Jesus! I'm sorry — I thought you meant the other one.

BARNABY: Are you making fun of me?

HEATHER: Yes.

BARNABY: We get used to that in Hollywood. But you *have* disappointed me.

HEATHER: How?

BARNABY: I did think the book was only pretend-fiction. I thought it all actually happened.

HEATHER: You're like me, Grace, you take things too seriously.
        [OLIVER *walks onto the veranda.*]

OLIVER: All clear.

BARNABY: Shall I pitch the film now?

OLIVER: Mr. Hosani needs a rest.

HEATHER: From what?

OLIVER: I know him, luv. He needs a bit of time. He's in a mood.

BARNABY: You seemed in a hurry.

HEATHER: I am. Desperately. Have you written songs? Is there a score? Do you have a tape?

BARNABY: Yes.
        [*He holds a tape up.*]
        Here.

HEATHER: There's a cassette player in the kitchen.

OLIVER: We'll set it up.
        [*He takes* BARNABY's *arm and leads him towards the kitchen.*]

BARNABY: I feel very odd. This island is odd.

HEATHER: Are you frightened?

BARNABY: Not since Jesus.
        [OLIVER *and* BARNABY *go into the kitchen.*]

HEATHER: How can anybody not be frightened?
        [*She sits on the floor next to* DANIEL's *chair and takes* DANIEL's *hand.*]

        I wish you could tell me something. Anything. It's not even that I think you're wise, or ever were. I just need you. I can't focus. I don't know what to worry about

first. Dylan going to Paris. Dylan upstairs with that
girl. Dylan getting nuked. Dylan getting AIDS. Dylan
getting religion. The remains of my own system. The
world cracking in half. Dylan doesn't think I'm
playing with a full deck. When I told him that I
worried about the destruction of the rain forests
because someday *he* might wake up without oxygen,
he was about to have me committed. I've gotten to the
point where I can't even have a meal without panic. I
had lunch at an outdoor restaurant last week. I looked
at the menu. I could not order eggs because they
cause heart attacks. I could not order chicken because
they are injected with dangerous antibiotics. I could
not order meat because livestock have eaten contaminated grass. I could not order fruit because they have
been sprayed with deadly chemicals. I could not order
vegetables because the produce in that town looked
extra-large as though it had mutated from the fallout.
I could not order bread because yeast is now thought
to damage the immune system. I could not order fish
because the waters they swim in are contaminated. I
sat there clawing at the menu, crying, laughing and
screaming at the same time, aware that there was one
indisputable fact — I was *hungry* and I didn't know
what to do about it. Then I realized I was having this
mini-breakdown outside, in the afternoon sun, and
now that the ozone layer has been destroyed, the
afternoon sun is slowly killing us. So I calmed down and
had a banana split. What the hell. It's immaterial for
me, anyway — I'm here courtesy of chemotherapy. I
have only seconds left. But the kids, the kids ... What
can they eat? What can they breathe? Who can they
sleep with? Sometimes I feel so guilty for bringing
Dylan into this mess. Oh shit, Danny, can't you tell
me something? You don't care anyhow. Look what
you've done to yourself. You know who had the right
idea? Mrs. Honey. Mrs. Foster, that is. Crusty old
dame. Do you remember her letter? What *do* you
remember? She wrote to us both from India. From
Goa. Did you ever read it? I've saved mine. She said
her travels finally took her to Goa and by then she
found the entire world was off its rocker, not just
America. Someone told her that if you lost your

passport in Goa, the police put you into the local madhouse until you could prove who you were. Well, that appealed to her. Amused her. She thought it was the first intelligent thing she had heard in years. So she tore up her passport and retired gracefully — into Bedlam. She's still there. Both her children have died. But she has never been ill, a fact that must seem quite logical in a madhouse. She sends me a postcard every summer. She must send one to you too. Does Oliver read them to you? She loved being Mrs. Honey. Even though you left out the important stuff.

[*Pause.*]

I wish you could tell me something, something to make me feel less afraid.

[*Pause.*]

Anything.

[*Pause.*]

DANIEL: Apple sauce.

[*Pause.*]

HEATHER: Thanks, kiddo. Thanks a lot. I was losing my nerve. I have something to do and I was losing my nerve. But apple sauce really helps. I needed that.

[HEATHER *rises and walks into the kitchen.*]

[*Blackout.*]

The Greek melody that DANIEL *was humming plays in the distance.*

The lights rise. One hour later.

DANIEL *is sitting in another chair on the veranda. Voices are heard in the kitchen.* ALIKI *walks out of the kitchen. She sees the map on the floor. She picks it up and looks at it.*

ALIKI: Maps. Ah so. Ah yes. Interesting.

[*She traces her finger on the map.*]

Here we are. Little island. Funny little island. Looks like no place else. Like moon.

[*She goes to* DANIEL.]

You do not eat? Jesus Man in kitchen talking and talking and talking. Makes me very not interested. Jesus Man serve purpose. Now Jesus Man kaput. You understand? Later you understand. I read your book.

Why you not say the King no good, why you not say
the Colonels come in the next year, why you not say
Greece in pain? You understand country in pain? I
think maybe not.

[DYLAN *enters.*]

DYLAN: Hey.

[*He kisses* ALIKI — *she moves away.*]

Come here . . .

ALIKI: Yes?

DYLAN: I leave, like, for the airport in a few hours.

ALIKI: So bye bye.

DYLAN: Come with me.

ALIKI: I promise to go to Crete.

DYLAN: That creep, like, doesn't even notice you. Why do you
want to be with him?

ALIKI: I make promise.

DYLAN: Break promise.

ALIKI: No. I have reason. So I go to Crete. But I leave Crete
tomorrow and fly to Athens. I meet you tomorrow in
Athens.

DYLAN: Meet me tomorrow in Paris.

ALIKI: No. Athens. Make Paris day later.

DYLAN: I can't. It's business.

ALIKI: Make Paris day later.

DYLAN: Has my Mom, like, put you up to this?

ALIKI: No. Your body.

[*She runs her hand across his chest.*]

DYLAN: Jeez!

ALIKI: This is true. You know what we do in Athens?

DYLAN: I think so.

ALIKI: You so sure?

DYLAN: Tell me.

[ALIKI, *aware that* DANIEL *is listening, whispers into*
DYLAN*'s ear.* DYLAN*'s eyes widen.*]

Sweet Aunt Lizzie!

ALIKI: And then . . .

[*She whispers into his ear again.*]

DYLAN: What's that?

ALIKI: Greek words.

DYLAN: What do they mean?

ALIKI: You make computer. With languages. Look it up.

[DYLAN *takes a tiny computer out of his pocket.*]

DYLAN: This is it. This is my baby.

ALIKI: Look words up.

DYLAN: Say them again.

> [ALIKI *whispers into his ear.*]

O.K. Now — press Greek. Press letters. Press
English. Then . . .

> [*He stares at the computer.*]

Holy shit!

ALIKI: You make Paris one day later?

> [*Pause.*]

Well?

DYLAN: I'll change the appointment. One day.

ALIKI: We meet at Cafe Homer in Plaka. Six-o-clock.

DYLAN: How do I, like, know you'll be there?

ALIKI: I be there.

DYLAN: Yeah, but how do I know?

ALIKI: I prove it to you. Wait.

> [ALIKI *runs off.* DYLAN *walks over to* DANIEL.]

DYLAN: Hey — Danny . . . there's this thing in your book — I
never read it, but that's only because I don't read
books but Mom told me the story and there's this guy
who's supposed to be you but he's not really you
although he sort of is, you know, and Mom says he
has, like, fears about sex and, like, I thought, hey,
that's crazy, nobody's got that no more, but I tell you
something — this girl is wild, this girl scares me —
I'm over my head, like. You know what I mean?

DANIEL: Don't sneeze.

DYLAN: What?

DANIEL: Don't sneeze.

DYLAN: What's that mean?

DANIEL: Don't sneeze.

DYLAN: What the fuck does that mean?

DANIEL: Don't sneeze.

DYLAN: Maybe I can invent a computer that can translate
your mind, huh?

> [HEATHER *and* BARNABY *walk in from the kitchen.*]

Don't tell Mom we had this talk.

BARNABY: I'm very nerves-orientated.

HEATHER: Pardon?

BARNABY: Scared shitless.

HEATHER: Don't be.

> [OLIVER *enters from the kitchen with a glass of orange juice
> and brings it to* DANIEL.]

BARNABY: Do you think he'll like my presentation? Will we effect a compatibility relationship? Will he even understand what I'm saying?

HEATHER: Don't worry about it.

OLIVER: [*to* DANIEL] Here's some fresh orange juice.

HEATHER: Just come with me.

OLIVER: I want you to drink it. You're not getting enough nourishment. Don't give me that glum face.

[HEATHER *leads* BARNABY *to* DANIEL.]

HEATHER: Danny — this is Barnaby Grace.

OLIVER: Drink the orange juice, luv, don't be difficult.

HEATHER: Mr. Grace is a very important film producer from California.

[DANIEL *stares straight ahead.*]

BARNABY: He's not looking at me.

HEATHER: Doesn't matter. Mr. Grace wants to make a film of 'A Table for a King'. I've asked him here to speak to you . . .

BARNABY: I can't tell you what an important moment this is for me, Mr. Hosani . . .

OLIVER: Will you please drink the juice?

BARNABY: I've wanted to meet you since I was fifteen.

[DANIEL *drinks the orange juice.*]

OLIVER: That's a good boy. All down.

BARNABY: I have a deep empathy syndrome with your work.

OLIVER: I think he wants to nap.

HEATHER: He can nap later.

[OLIVER *takes* DANIEL*'s pulse.*]

OLIVER: He's tired.

HEATHER: He's not tired.

OLIVER: I don't like his pulses.

HEATHER: I adore his pulses.

OLIVER: He needs a nap.

HEATHER: There's no time.

DYLAN: Mom, maybe he does, like, need to rest.

HEATHER: Shouldn't you be packing for Paris?

[DYLAN *holds his hands up in the air.*]

DYLAN: Hey! Hey! Hey!

HEATHER: Barnaby is leaving in a few hours as well. It has to be now.

OLIVER: Just a short nap.

HEATHER: No dice.

[OLIVER *pulls her away from* DANIEL.]

Ouch!

OLIVER: What's got into you?

HEATHER: Stop protecting him.

OLIVER: I'm paid to protect him. He mustn't hear about this film. It will distress him.

HEATHER: Can't be helped.

OLIVER: What the hell are you doing?

      [HEATHER *returns to* DANIEL.]

HEATHER: Barnaby is going to tell us about the film.

BARNABY: Well, Mr. Hosani, as I see this project, and I consider it from the very start, a go project . . . [*to* HEATHER] He's not looking at me.

HEATHER: He can hear.

BARNABY: My strong point is eye contact.

HEATHER: Trust in Jesus.

BARNABY: Oh. Yes. Well — O.K. . . .

HEATHER: But condense.

BARNABY: Yes. Yes.

      [ALIKI *enters. She is carrying a bag. She stops, then sits down and watches* BARNABY.]

Mr. Hosani, I truly respect your book and I want to treat it with love, because Jesus says love is the answer . . .

HEATHER: *Condense.*

BARNABY: Oh. Yes. I see your book in a positive light. As a life-affirmer rather than a down-in-the-dumpser. And music can help, because it's difficult for an audience to focus on a story any more without a strong sound-track and a lot of quick images, a lot of fast brain messages, and, of course, you will have a very generous financial cut of the album . . ..

HEATHER: Tell him about Mabel.

BARNABY: Oh. Mabel. Mabel is one of those roles that comes along once in a lifetime.

DYLAN: You never told me about a Mabel, Mom.

BARNABY: Mabel is Mrs. Honey. She needs a first name, and, of course, I've made her younger, about thirty. You see, there have to be a few slight alterations. I've conducted several market surveys on aspects of the plot. Mabel, for instance, will have a very tender romance with David — I have to cut the gay stuff, the market won't hold that post-AIDS — and Jesus is wary of it, anyway — and David's not Jewish any

more, even though Judaism was an initial interest of
Jesus, we find there's low audience concern for the
subject, so then the waiter who seduces David
becomes, of course, a waitress, and that scene is a
blessing in terms of soundtrack, all those old sixties'
hits — but the *essence* of your story remains exactly the
same, even though now it's a young boy who falls in
love with a slightly older woman, played by a major
star, who he betrays ultimately — and yes, that is the
down side — but wait! — the think-positive aspect is
that she never gives up her position about the table,
which is a lesson to all of us about holding on to our
beliefs, this is, in fact, a movie about holding on to our
beliefs, and thus a modern parable for the Crucifixion,
which was the ultimate hold-on, wasn't it? — and it
climaxes in the film in a song that I know will be not
just a song, but a megasong, and most important,
a megasong with a message — which ends with —
here . . .
        [*He reaches for the tape recorder.*]
This is the music . . .
        [*He switches the tape recorder on — a piano is playing.*]
And you'll have to excuse my voice, but I want to give
you some idea —
        [*He sings to the music.*]
'They can woe me.
They can charm me.
They can hurt me.
They can harm me.
They can send in
An army.
But as long as I am able
I won't give up my table
Or my name's not Mabel
No —
I won't give up
I won't give up
I won't give up
Not even for
A King.'
        [*He turns the tape recorder off.*]
Now I know you're probably asking how can we hold
the interest of a modern audience for so long with just

one woman singing plot — well, let me throw this to
you, bit by bit — I promise you we will not lose the
concentration factor — we're going to have a series of
quick images. Here, I'll break it down. 'They can woe
me. They can charm me' — short shots of Mabel
being courted by about a hundred waiters — it's a
hotel now, not an inn — O.K.? 'They can hurt me,
They can harm me' — Mabel being tortured. 'They
can send in an army' — a shot of an *entire* army — we'll
film it in some country with lots of cheap labour, so
don't worry. 'But as long as I am able, I won't give up
my table' — a fantasy sequence of Mabel at her table
and aging, growing older and older — which has
appeal for citizens-in-retirement. 'Or my name's not
Mabel' — this is beautiful, we bring in the animators
to draw the name Mabel, surrounded by stars and
moons and little birds and squirrels. 'No — I won't
give up, I won't give up, I won't give up, Not even for
a King' — a long pan of Mabel holding onto the table
through a gale-force wind, surrounded by the army
and the waiters and the King and the entire Royal
Household! So you see, for those who are not listening
orientated, there's plenty of visual dividends, and the
essence of your message, that a little wooden table
can be worth fighting for against all the big boys, will
be given a new strength and power and will resound,
not unlike the Gospels, through the ages, forever and
ever.

[*Silence.*]

DYLAN: Holy shit.

[DANIEL *stands up.*]

HEATHER: Danny!

BARNABY: Mr. Hosani — is it a go?

DANIEL: Oysters!

[DANIEL *starts to choke* BARNABY.]

[OLIVER *tries to pull* DANIEL *away.*]

OLIVER: Come on, luv, let's stop this now . . .

DANIEL: Oysters! I park you, I park you.

OLIVER: It's alright, luv, it's alright . . .

DANIEL: He is bluesing me, he is bluesing me . . .

OLIVER: It's alright . . . let's take our hands away . . . let's calm
down . . .

[*He pulls* DANIEL *away from* BARNABY.]
That's right . . . that's a good boy . . . come on, now . . .
no tears . . .
[*He leads* DANIEL *to a chair.*]

DANIEL: Canasta. Canasta.

BARNABY: There's a tension-factor here I wasn't prepared for.

HEATHER: Don't worry.

BARNABY: Stop telling me not to worry.

HEATHER: You have a deal.

BARNABY: What?

HEATHER: You have a deal. Phone my lawyer when you get back
to the States. The book is yours.

BARNABY: Blessed Jesus!

HEATHER: Indeed. But I think you better pack. Get to your boat
early.

BARNABY: The Lord's been with me, he's my shepherd, he's
clinched my deal . . .

HEATHER: Please go. Just go.

BARNABY: O.K. Thank you.
[*He runs off, patting* ALIKI *on the head as he does so.*]
Come on, sunshine, we're leaving.

HEATHER: He restoreth my soul. Ha!
[*She starts to shake — lights a cigarette.*]

OLIVER: [*to* DANIEL] Now you mustn't weep — it's all going to
be alright.
[*He brings over a needle.*]
I'm just giving you a needle.

DYLAN: Mom, what's wrong with you?

HEATHER: Nothing.

DYLAN: You shouldn't smoke.

HEATHER: You shouldn't go to Paris.

DYLAN: Lay off.
[ALIKI *goes to* DYLAN. *She removes a jewel box from her
bag and holds it out towards him.*]
What's that?

ALIKI: A box for jewels. Mine.

DYLAN: Oh?
[ALIKI *removes a bracelet from her arm.*]

ALIKI: I take my bracelet . . .
[*She puts the bracelet into the box.*]
I put it inside.
[*She removes a ring from her finger.*]

And my ring.

[*She places the ring in the box.*]

Inside.

DYLAN: Yeah?

[ALIKI *hands him the box.*]

ALIKI: And I give to you.

DYLAN: Why?

ALIKI: So you return it to me in Athens. So you know I keep my promise.

DYLAN: I can't, like, take this.

ALIKI: The problem, I think, is not if I meet you in Athens. The problem, I think, is if you meet me. Now you have to. Yes?

[ALIKI *kisses* DYLAN *and exits.*]

[OLIVER *has put a needle into* DANIEL*'s forehead.*]

OLIVER: There, that's better, isn't it? That's much better.

[HEATHER *looks over at* DANIEL.]

HEATHER: Shit, Oliver, did you give him a needle?

OLIVER: Yes.

HEATHER: Will it put him to sleep?

OLIVER: Soon.

HEATHER: But he needs to feel *something*, even if it's anger . . .

[*She goes to* DANIEL.]

Danny, I've sold your book.

OLIVER: Leave it alone now, luv.

HEATHER: It's going to sing and dance, kiddo. You've invented a Mabel.

OLIVER: Just leave it alone.

HEATHER: That idiot will make hash out of it.

DYLAN: Hey, Mom, maybe he shouldn't hear this.

HEATHER: Danny, the book is bullshit.

DYLAN: Mom . . .

[*He grabs her hand.*]

OLIVER: Take her away, Dylan.

HEATHER: Hands off! The book is bullshit. You didn't tell the truth. About the dentist. About the waiter. About you. Too contentious, too political, too blatant, too unpopular. You said an artist has to select. Well, your selections took you right into the pages of *Vogue*. And no doubt you're right, if Mrs. Honey babbled on about atomic bombs, it would have seemed far too obvious and she wouldn't have been in the least endearing. And if the waiter had whispered sweet nothings about Marx and Lenin into your ear while you were making love, as he did, instead of singing sixties' pop songs, it would have lost its universal touch, I suppose, and the readers would have had to deal with the fact that by the time the book was published that kid was probably in prison being tortured, and that ain't 'Book of the Month Club', is it? And I know, I know your lies look more like truth than the truth itself, and I know that my way it would actually have been diminished, but Danny, maybe if you had just tried it, Dylan wouldn't be going to Paris today.

DYLAN: Leave me out of this, you hear?

HEATHER: We tell such lies, Danny. Now that idiot is going to take your artful lies and make them artless, that's all.

DANIEL: Ocean.

HEATHER: Yes — ocean — you understand, don't you? I had to do it. For both of us.

DANIEL: Ocean.

HEATHER: For the money.

DANIEL: Ocean.

HEATHER: You forgive me, don't you?

DANIEL: Ocean . . .

> [*He closes his eyes.*]

HEATHER: Danny, forgive me.

OLIVER: He's asleep, luv.

HEATHER: [*shouts*] Why did you give him that goddamn needle?

> [*She starts to cough and gasp — cannot catch her breath.*]

DYLAN: Hey — Mom . . .

OLIVER: Let it out, luv . . .

HEATHER: I'm alright, I'm alright, don't crowd me, leave me alone . . . I just can't catch my breath . . .

> [OLIVER *signals to* DYLAN *to give her air. She calms down.*]

There . . . it's alright . . .

DYLAN: Hey, Oliver, I think maybe . . .

> [*He signals toward the needles.*]

OLIVER: Yes. Good idea.

DYLAN: Come on, Mom, sit down.

> [*He takes her to a chair.*]

HEATHER: I've left word with the lawyers. The film will bring in a fortune. It's all going to the right organizations, all of it. It will be written in the contract. The money

will go to fight against nuclear energy, against political oppression, against AIDS, against religious
extremism — I've spread it over nineteen important
groups . . .

DYLAN: Right, Mom.

HEATHER: I had to do something good with our lives. Everything
seems so wasted.

OLIVER: Here, luv, just one . . .

[*He places a needle in her forehead.*]

HEATHER: If only I knew how to get to Goa.

DYLAN: It's alright, Mom . . .

HEATHER: If only I could stop smoking.

DYLAN: It's alright . . .

HEATHER: Shit . . . Dylan . . . I've done it wrong, haven't I?
I've given the money to too many groups. I'm still
unfocused. Maybe just two or three. I've done it
wrong . . .

DYLAN: It's alright.

HEATHER: There's just so much to worry about, so much . . .

[*She closes her eyes.*]

DYLAN: Sure, Mom.

HEATHER: Ocean.

DYLAN: What?

HEATHER: Ocean . . .

[*She falls asleep.*]

DYLAN: Boy, this stuff really works.

OLIVER: It causes a deep sleep for one hour. A very restful
sleep. Just one hour. It's cleansing.

DYLAN: Yeah? Hey — do you think? . . . Well, I don't have to
go to the airport for another two hours. And I'm very
tense.

[*He sits on the floor.*]

I mean, I don't, like, get tense a lot. I don't worry like
my Mom. Or my Dad. She don't see too much of my
Dad in me and that, like, upsets her. He was this poet
from Chile. I don't remember him much, they weren't
together too long. There was some sort of revolution
there, in Chile, and he went back, and then there was
this takeover, like, and they arrested him because of
his poetry and they put him in a stadium and they
threw kerosene on him and set him on fire. Mom
thinks I should get into politics because of that, but
that isn't, like, a positive example, you know what I

mean, and actually, in its way, that's what turned me towards computers. I mean, I didn't know the guy and that was his scene, not mine, it don't have nothin' to do with me. Who needs kerosene, huh? I guess I should read a printout of his poems someday. See, I've got this IQ for technical things that's really incredible and I can make, like, a lot of money by the end of this week, and I have this unbelievable girl meeting me tomorrow, and all that's enough for me to handle; in fact, I think she's, like, too much to handle, so one hour of, like, sleep, Ollie . . .

[OLIVER *places a needle into his forehead.*]

Ouch. I thought you didn't feel it.

OLIVER: Only when it goes into the head of a genius.

DYLAN: I mean, what do you think of Aliki?

OLIVER: Don't know.

DYLAN: Danny kept saying something about her.

DYLAN: What?

DYLAN: "Don't sneeze." I wonder what that meant?

OLIVER: Don't know.

DYLAN: I'm tired. Do you think I'll, like, say ocean too?

[*He closes his eyes.*]

OLIVER: I doubt it, Dylan?

[OLIVER *touches him.* DYLAN *is asleep.* OLIVER *looks at* DYLAN, *then at* HEATHER *and* DANIEL. *They are all asleep, with needles in their foreheads.*]

Rest, my little chicks. Rest.

[OLIVER *takes a cassette player from the table. He sits in the rocking chair. He puts the headphones on and turns the machine on. He rocks gently, listening to music and closes his eyes.*]

[BARNABY *and* ALIKI *enter, with their suitcases. They look at the others.* BARNABY *is about to try to speak to them but* ALIKI *shakes her head 'no' and points him to the door. They walk to the front door.* BARNABY *leaves.* ALIKI *starts to follow him then stops and walks back into the room. She stares at* DANIEL, HEATHER, DYLAN *and* OLIVER.]

[*The lights fade on the room, except for one bright light on* ALIKI, *a look of utter contempt on her face.*]

[*Blackout.*]

Church bells.

The lights rise. Four days later.

OLIVER *is sitting in the rocking chair. He is not listening to music.*

DANIEL *walks in, slowly, with difficulty. He walks onto the veranda.* OLIVER *doesn't look up.*

There is a low, rumbling noise, off, in the distance.

OLIVER: Well, look who's up and about. Feeling better, are we? That's a good boy. Slept well, eh? Four whole days. That's a record for you. Eyes open to take a little nourishment, then back shut into never-never land. Four days.

    [DANIEL *sits down.*]

Sitting down, are we, luv? That's good. Do you hear that noise? Like thunder. In the distance. Spoils the peaceful drone of the rainfall. Hasn't stopped raining. You didn't miss any sun.

    [*He looks at* DANIEL.]

I guess we were depressed, weren't we? Does your face have more colour in it? Probably. We like our sleep.

    [*Pause — he looks away.*]

Well — what have you missed? A lot. You've missed a lot.

    [*Pause.*]

Heather's in the hospital. She had a choking fit as soon as Dylan left. That's when you went to sleep, wasn't it? Yes.

    [*Pause.*]

The cancer has crawled up through her system and is surrounding her windpipe. Leaning on it, actually. Do you want to hear this? Do you want to go back to sleep? They think they can reduce it a bit. They figure she has a few weeks. But you know Heather, she'll turn weeks into months, if she can. I have a lot of time for Heather. I'm just afraid the fight may leave her when she hears about Dylan.

    [*Pause.*]

Are you sure you don't want to go back to sleep? I'm not giving you a needle. Not now.

    [*Pause.*]

Dylan's plane exploded. Everyone dead. A bomb. Hardly got into the air. Just over the crater. They found some wreckage. On the cliffs. The explosive device had been placed in a little jewel box. Pretty clever, eh?

[*Pause.*]

Are you tired again? What is that sound? I liked Dylan. Did you? It was Aliki, of course. Except her name's not Aliki. It's Maria something-or-other and she's not Greek, she's Lebanese. Did you suspect something, you little devil? "Don't sneeze"? What did that mean? A Palestinian courier had been booked on that flight, that's supposedly who she was after. He cancelled at the last moment. They're not sure if she belonged to a Muslim extremist group or another Palestinian faction or the Israeli secret service. Or the CIA. Or the KGB. My guess is all of the above. Well, doesn't matter really, does it? Another gesture for freedom, no matter how you squeeze it.

[*Pause.*]

They traced Aliki-or-Maria to Crete. Well, I could have told them that's where she was. She and Barnaby had taken a hotel room. They found Barnaby. His throat was cut. Aliki-Maria has disappeared.

[*Pause.*]

Thin air.

[*Pause.*]

Well, you can take some comfort in the knowledge that your book will never be a musical now. Assuming it upsets you at all.

[*Pause.*]

I know the world at large would consider you a total mess, but I rather think you lead a charmed life. I'm not giving you a needle. What is that noise?

[*Pause.*]

I'm leaving you. I've placed an advertisement in the *Herald-Tribune* for a replacement. I'll find you someone very convivial. It seems that I myself am on a sinking ship. I'm waving goodbye as well. Do you understand? I found a lesion on my arm. I had the necessary tests. I have AIDS. I suppose it can be classified as ironic. The last time I was with someone was five years ago. And only for a minute. Well — so it goes.

[*Pause.*]

It hasn't registered yet, really. I'm numb. I'm not even angry or sad. Just numb. Funny, that.

[*Pause.*]

But I am quite sure of one thing and that's that I'm not ending my days with you.

[*Pause.*]

I used to work in a clinic. Didn't get paid well. But it meant something. It helped. I have healing gifts. Don't I, luv? I think I've been wasting them on you. But right now, with this odd numbness, everything seems wasted.

[*Pause.*]

I don't hate you. Don't think that. But if you have gifts, you should use them, shouldn't you? It's a way of facing the madness and shouting 'stop'. You, of course, can't even say 'stop'. If you tried, it would come out as ice-cream.

[*Pause.*]

So you've missed a lot. It pays to stay awake these days.

[*Pause.*]

What stories are you writing in your head? What faces do you see? Do the heavens dance? Does a star fall on Albania? Do you feel the cool breeze from the Levant? Does the breeze comfort you? Do you know at last what it means?

[*Pause.*]

What is that noise?

[*The sound grows louder.*]

[DANIEL *rises. He walks to the edge of the veranda. He stares out at the sea.*]

DANIEL: Apricot.

OLIVER: What?

DANIEL: The apricot is erupting.

[*The noise grows very loud.*]

[DANIEL *starts to laugh.*]

THE END